The Ultimate Ninja Double Stack XL Air Fryer Cookbook for UK

Crispy & Mouthwatering Simple Recipes | The Ultimate Guide to Double Stack XL Air Fryer Tips & Tricks | FULL-COLOR-EDITION

Summer Pritchard

© Copyright 2024
- All Rights Reserved

The content contained within this book may not be reproduced, duplicated or transmitted without direct written permission from the author or the publisher.

Under no circumstances will any blame or legal responsibility be held against the publisher, or author, for any damages, reparation, or monetary loss due to the information contained within this book, either directly or indirectly.

Legal Notice:

This book is copyright protected. It is only for personal use. You cannot amend, distribute, sell, use, quote or paraphrase any part, or the content within this book, without the consent of the author or publisher.

Disclaimer Notice:

Please note the information contained within this document is for educational and entertainment purposes only. All effort has been executed to present accurate, up to date, reliable, complete information. No warranties of any kind are declared or implied. Readers acknowledge that the author is not engaged in the rendering of legal, financial, medical or professional advice. The content within this book has been derived from various sources. Please consult a licensed professional before attempting any techniques outlined in this book.

By reading this document, the reader agrees that under no circumstances is the author responsible for any losses, direct or indirect, that are incurred as a result of the use of the information contained within this document, including, but not limited to, errors, omissions, or inaccuracies.

CONTENTS

01   Introduction

02   Fundamentals of Ninja DoubleStack XL 2-Basket Air Fryer

09   4-Week Meal Plan

11   Chapter 1 Breakfast

17   Chapter 2 Vegetables and Sides

27   Chapter 3 Snacks and Starters

33   Chapter 4 Poultry

39   Chapter 5 Fish and Seafood

44   Chapter 6 Beef, Pork, and Lamb

57   Chapter 7 Desserts

64   Conclusion

65   Appendix 1 Measurement Conversion Chart

66   Appendix 2 Air Fryer Cooking Chart

67   Appendix 3 Recipes Index

Introduction

Welcome to the Ninja DoubleStack XL 2-Basket Air Fryer Cookbook! This cookbook is designed to help you get the most out of your versatile and powerful Ninja air fryer. With its dual-basket design, you can prepare multiple dishes at once, making meal preparation quicker and more efficient than ever. Whether you are a busy professional, a parent juggling numerous responsibilities, or someone who simply enjoys the convenience of modern cooking technology, this cookbook will become an invaluable resource in your kitchen.

Inside, you'll find a collection of delicious and nutritious recipes that cater to a variety of tastes and dietary preferences. From crispy starters and mouth-watering mains to delectable desserts, we've got you covered. Each recipe has been carefully crafted to maximise the use of your air fryer, ensuring you achieve perfect results every time. Additionally, we've included handy tips and tricks to help you master your air fryer and elevate your cooking skills.

Embrace the convenience and health benefits of air frying with the Ninja DoubleStack XL 2-Basket Air Fryer. Enjoy preparing meals with less oil and faster cooking times, all while maintaining the delicious flavours and textures you love. Let's embark on a culinary adventure together and make every meal a delight!

Fundamentals of Ninja DoubleStack XL 2-Basket Air Fryer

The Ninja DoubleStack XL 2-Basket Air Fryer is a cutting-edge kitchen appliance designed to simplify and enhance your cooking experience. At its core, the air fryer uses powerful hot air circulation to cook food evenly and efficiently, allowing you to achieve a crispy, fried texture with significantly less oil compared to traditional frying methods. This not only makes your meals healthier but also reduces the mess and hassle associated with deep frying.

One of the standout features of the Ninja DoubleStack XL is its dual-basket design. This innovative setup allows you to cook two different dishes simultaneously, making it perfect for preparing complete meals in one go. Each basket can operate independently with its own temperature and timing settings, providing maximum versatility and convenience. Whether you're cooking for a family dinner or entertaining guests, this feature ensures that your food is ready at the same time, hot and fresh from the fryer.

Additionally, the air fryer boasts a generous capacity, ideal for larger households or batch cooking. It also comes equipped with multiple cooking functions, including air fry, roast, reheat, and dehydrate, making it a multi-functional tool in your culinary arsenal. With the Ninja DoubleStack XL 2-Basket Air Fryer, you can enjoy delicious, healthier meals with ease and efficiency.

What is Ninja DoubleStack XL 2-Basket Air Fryer?

The Ninja DoubleStack XL 2-Basket Air Fryer represents a significant leap forward in kitchen technology, combining convenience with versatility to elevate your culinary capabilities. Its standout feature, the dual-zone design, allows for simultaneous cooking of two distinct dishes, making it an ideal choice for busy households or those who love to entertain. The spacious capacity ensures ample room for preparing generous portions, catering effortlessly to family meals or gatherings with friends.

At the heart of its operation lies advanced air frying technology, which not only ensures even cooking but also reduces oil usage significantly compared to traditional frying methods. This not only promotes healthier eating habits but also retains the delicious flavours and textures that make every dish a delight. The independent operation of each basket enables precise control over cooking conditions, allowing you to synchronise timings and temperatures seamlessly for perfectly coordinated meals.

The Ninja DoubleStack XL offers a variety of cooking presets tailored to different culinary needs, from air frying and roasting to reheating, dehydrating, and baking. This versatility is complemented by an intuitive digital control panel that simplifies adjustments and provides clear feedback on cooking progress. Moreover, the dishwasher-safe non-stick baskets and crisper plates streamline cleanup, ensuring that enjoying your meal is the main focus rather than washing up.

Whether you're crafting crispy fries, succulent roasts, or delicate pastries, this air fryer is engineered to deliver consistent, high-quality results with efficiency and ease. It empowers you to explore new recipes and cooking techniques while promoting a healthier lifestyle through reduced oil consumption. The Ninja DoubleStack XL 2-Basket Air Fryer isn't just a kitchen appliance; it's a partner in culinary exploration, making every mealtime an opportunity to create memorable dishes that delight and satisfy.

Benefits of Using it

The Ninja DoubleStack XL 2-Basket Air Fryer offers numerous benefits that make it an essential addition to any kitchen. Here are some key advantages:

1. Dual-Basket Design
One of the standout features of this air fryer is its dual-basket design. This allows you to cook two different dishes simultaneously, saving time and effort. Whether you're preparing a main course and a side dish or cooking for different dietary preferences, the dual-basket design offers unmatched flexibility.

2. Healthier Cooking
Air frying is known for its ability to cook food with significantly less oil compared to traditional frying methods. This means you can enjoy your favourite crispy dishes with fewer calories and less fat, making it a healthier option for you and your family.

3. Time Efficiency
The DoubleStack XL 2-Basket Air Fryer heats up quickly and cooks food faster than traditional ovens. Its dual-zone technology lets you set different temperatures and cooking times for each basket, ensuring that your dishes are perfectly timed to be ready simultaneously. This efficiency is perfect for busy households and those who want to spend less time in the kitchen.

4. Versatility
This air fryer is not just for frying. It can roast, bake, reheat, and dehydrate, offering a wide range of cooking options. From crispy chips and roasted vegetables to baked goods and dehydrated fruits, the possibilities are endless.

5. Ease of Use and Cleaning
The intuitive controls and digital display make it easy to set the temperature and cooking time accurately. Additionally, the baskets and crisper plates are non-stick and dishwasher safe, ensuring a hassle-free cleaning process.

6. Large Capacity
With its XL size, this air fryer can handle larger portions, making it ideal for families or when entertaining guests. You can prepare a complete meal in one go, reducing the need for multiple cooking appliances.

The Ninja DoubleStack XL 2-Basket Air Fryer offers health benefits, time-saving convenience, versatility, and ease of use, making it a valuable tool for any kitchen. Enjoy delicious, healthier meals with less effort and more creativity.

Function Buttons

Air Fry: Use this function to achieve a crispy and crunchy texture for your food with minimal to no oil.
Air Broil: Add the crispy finishing touch to meals, or melt toppings to create the perfect finish.
Bake: Create decadent baked treats and desserts.
Roast: Utilize the unit as an oven to cook tender meats and other dishes.
Reheat: Revive leftovers by gently warming them, resulting in crispy, delicious outcomes.
Dehydrate: Dehydrate meats, fruits, and vegetables to create healthy snacks.
Power Button: This button turns the unit on and also shuts it off, stopping all cooking functions.

Operating Buttons

Control Zone 1: Control the output for the top zone (Zone 1).
Control Zone 2: Control the output for the bottom zone (Zone 2).
Crisper Plate Position:
Lower Position (Bottom of Basket): Allows air to surround food for even cooking and crisping. For proper placement, make sure the cutouts are on the left and right sides of the basket.
Upper Position (Elevated in Basket): For better browning and grilling results, use the upper position. Place the crisper plate in the basket with the cutouts facing the front and back of the basket.
Temp Button: Press the TEMP button, then turn the dial to adjust the cooking temperature before or during cooking.
Time Button: Press the TIME button, then turn the dial to adjust the cook time in any function before or during the cook cycle.
Double Stack Pro: Cook 4 foods at once in 2 independent air fry baskets for evenly crispy meals and snacks.
SMART FINISH Button: Automatically syncs the cook times to ensure both zones finish at the same time, even if they have different cook times.
MATCH COOK Button: Automatically matches Zone 2 settings to those of Zone 1 to cook a larger amount of the same food or cook different foods using the same function, temperature, and time.
START/PAUSE Button: Rotate the dial from side to side to select the desired function. Start cooking by pressing the START/PAUSE button.
Hold Mode: "Hold" will appear on the unit while in SMART FINISH mode. One zone will be cooking, while the other zone will be holding

Fundamentals of Ninja DoubleStack XL 2-Basket Air Fryer

until the times sync together.
Standby Mode: If there is no interaction with the control panel for 10 minutes, the unit will enter standby mode.

Step-By-Step Ninja DoubleStack XL 2-Basket Air Fryer

Cooking with Double Stack Pro
The Double Stack Pro allows you to cook four foods at once in two independent baskets. You have the flexibility to cook in both zones or just in a single zone.

Using SMART FINISH or MATCH COOK:
When using these functions, press DOUBLE STACK PRO before pressing either SMART FINISH or MATCH COOK. If you are cooking in a single zone, press DOUBLE STACK PRO before pressing START/PAUSE.

Ending the Cook Time in One Zone (While Using Both Zones)

1. Select the zone you would like to stop.
2. Press START/PAUSE to end cooking.
3. When cooking is complete, the unit will beep and "COOL" will appear on the display for 60 seconds.

Pausing Cooking
Cooking will automatically pause when a basket is removed. Reinsert the basket to resume cooking.

When Using in SMART FINISH or MATCH COOK
If you remove a basket, the other basket will automatically pause to ensure cooking finishes simultaneously. Reinsert the basket to continue cooking in both zones.

Cooking with DualZone Technology

DualZone Technology utilises two cooking zones to increase versatility. The Sync feature ensures that, regardless of different cook settings, both zones will finish ready to serve at the same time.

Smart Finish
To finish cooking at the same time when foods have different cook times, temperatures, or even functions:
1. Place ingredients in the baskets, then insert baskets into the unit.
2. Select Zone 1. Select the desired cooking function using the dial. Press the TEMP button, then turn the dial to set the temperature, and press the TIME button, then turn the dial to set the time.
3. Select Zone 2, then select the desired cooking function using the dial. Press the TEMP button, then turn the dial to set the temperature, and use the TIME arrows to set the time.
4. Press SMART FINISH, then press START/PAUSE to begin cooking in the zone with the longest time. The other zone will display Hold. The unit will beep and activate the second zone when both zones have the same time remaining.
5. When cooking is complete, the unit will beep and "COOL" will appear on the display for 60 seconds.
6. Remove ingredients by tipping them out or using silicone-tipped tongs/utensils.

Match COOK
To cook a larger amount of the same food, or cook different foods using the same function, temperature, and time:
1. Place ingredients in the baskets, then insert baskets into the unit.
2. Select Zone 1. Select the desired cooking function using the dial. Press

the TEMP button, then turn the dial to set the temperature, and press the TIME button, then turn the dial to set the time.

3. Press the MATCH COOK button to copy the Zone 1 settings to Zone 2. Then press START/PAUSE to begin cooking in both zones.

4. When cooking is complete, the unit will beep and "COOL" will appear on the display for 60 seconds.

5. Remove ingredients by tipping them out or using silicone-tipped tongs/utensils.

Starting Both Zones at the Same Time, but Ending at Different Times

1. Select Zone 1, then select the desired function using the dial. Press the TEMP button, then turn the dial to set the temperature.
2. Press the TIME button, then turn the dial to set the time.
3. Select Zone 2 and repeat steps 1 and 2.
4. Press START/PAUSE to begin cooking in both zones.
5. When cooking is complete, the unit will beep and "COOL" will appear on the display for 60 seconds.
6. Remove ingredients by tipping them out or using silicone-tipped tongs/utensils.

Cooking in A Single Zone

To start using the unit, plug the power cord into a wall socket and press the power button.

Air Fry

1. Insert the crisper plate into the basket. Place your ingredients in the basket, then slide the basket into the unit.
2. Choose either Zone 1 or Zone 2. Turn the dial to select AIR FRY.
3. Press TEMP and adjust the temperature using the dial to your preferred setting.
4. Press TIME and adjust the cooking time in 1-minute increments, up to 1 hour. Press START/PAUSE to begin cooking.
5. Once cooking finishes, the unit will beep, and "COOL" will display for 60 seconds.
6. Remove your cooked ingredients by tipping them out or using silicone-tipped tongs/utensils.

Bake

1. If desired, insert the crisper plate into the basket. Place your ingredients in the basket and slide it into the unit.
2. Select Zone 1 or Zone 2. Turn the dial to choose BAKE.
3. Press TEMP and adjust the temperature using the dial to your desired setting.
4. Press TIME and set the cooking time in 1-minute increments up to 1 hour, or in 5-minute increments from 1 to 4 hours. Press START/PAUSE to start cooking.
5. After cooking completes, the unit will beep, and "COOL" will display for 60 seconds.
6. Remove your cooked ingredients by tipping them out or using silicone-tipped tongs/utensils.

Air Broil

1. Insert the crisper plate into the basket. Place your ingredients in the basket, then slide the basket into the unit.
2. Choose either Zone 1 or Zone 2. Turn the dial to select AIR BROIL.
3. The temperature is preset to 230°C. There is no temperature adjustment

available or necessary when using the Air Broil function.
Press TIME and set the cooking time in 1-minute increments, up to 30 minutes. Press START/PAUSE to begin cooking.
4. When cooking completes, the unit will beep, and "COOL" will display for 60 seconds.
5. Remove your cooked ingredients by tipping them out or using silicone-tipped tongs/utensils.

Reheat

1. Optionally, install the crisper plate in the basket. Place your ingredients in the basket and slide it into the unit.
2. Select Zone 1 or Zone 2. Turn the dial to choose REHEAT.
3. Press TEMP and adjust the temperature using the dial to your desired setting.
4. Press TIME and set the reheating time in 1-minute increments, up to 1 hour. Press START/PAUSE to begin reheating.
5. When the reheating process is complete, the unit will beep, and "COOL" will display for 60 seconds.
6. Remove your reheated ingredients by tipping them out or using silicone-tipped tongs/utensils.

Roast

1. Optionally, insert the crisper plate into the basket. Place your ingredients in the basket and slide it into the unit.
2. Select Zone 1 or Zone 2. Turn the dial to select ROAST.
3. Press TEMP and adjust the temperature using the dial to your desired setting.
4. Press TIME and set the cooking time in 1-minute increments up to 1 hour. Press START/PAUSE to begin cooking.
5. When roasting is complete, the unit will beep, and "COOL" will display for 60 seconds.
6. Remove your roasted ingredients by tipping them out or using silicone-tipped tongs/utensils.

Dehydrate

1. Arrange ingredients in a single layer in the basket. Install the crisper plate on top of the ingredients in the basket, then place another layer of ingredients on the crisper plate.
2. Select Zone 1 or Zone 2. Turn the dial to select DEHYDRATE. The default temperature will appear on the display.
3. Press TEMP and adjust the temperature using the dial to your desired setting.
4. Press TIME and set the dehydration time in 15-minute increments, from 1 to 12 hours. Press START/PAUSE to begin dehydrating.
5. When the dehydration process is complete, the unit will beep, and "COOL" will display for 60 seconds.
6. Remove your dehydrated ingredients by tipping them out or using silicone-tipped tongs/utensils.

Tips for Using Accessories
The Ninja DoubleStack XL 2-Basket Air Fryer comes with a range of accessories that enhance its functionality and make cooking a breeze. Here are some tips to help you get the most out of these accessories:
1. Crisper Plates
The crisper plates are essential for achieving that perfect, crispy texture on your chips, vegetables, and other fried favourites. Make sure to:
Arrange food evenly: Spread your food items in a single layer to ensure

even cooking and maximum crispiness.

Shake or turn halfway: For the best results, shake the basket or turn the food halfway through the cooking cycle.

2. Divider

The divider allows you to cook two different foods simultaneously without mixing flavours. To use it effectively:

Select compatible cooking functions: Ensure both items require similar cooking temperatures and times to avoid undercooking or overcooking.

Check doneness individually: Since different foods cook at different rates, monitor each side and adjust cooking times if necessary.

3. Baking Pan

The baking pan is perfect for cakes, casseroles, and other baked dishes. To make the most of it:

Preheat the air fryer: Preheating helps achieve better baking results.

Use parchment paper: Line the baking pan with parchment paper to prevent sticking and make cleanup easier.

4. Grill Plate

The grill plate is ideal for grilling meats, fish, and vegetables. Follow these tips for optimal grilling:

Preheat the grill plate: Allow the grill plate to preheat for a few minutes to get those beautiful grill marks and enhance flavour.

Oil the plate lightly: Brush a small amount of oil on the grill plate to prevent sticking and make flipping easier.

5. Skewers

Perfect for kebabs and skewered vegetables, the skewers can be used to create a variety of dishes. When using skewers:

Cut ingredients evenly: Ensure all pieces are of similar size for even cooking.

Rotate halfway: Turn the skewers halfway through the cooking process for uniform grilling.

By following these tips, you can make the most of the accessories that come with your Ninja DoubleStack XL 2-Basket Air Fryer and enjoy a wide range of delicious and perfectly cooked meals.

Cleaning and Caring for Your Ninja DoubleStack XL 2-Basket Air Fryer

Proper cleaning and maintenance of your Ninja DoubleStack XL 2-Basket Air Fryer are essential for ensuring its longevity and optimal performance. Follow these simple steps to keep your appliance in top condition:

Daily Cleaning

1. Unplug and Cool Down: Always ensure the air fryer is unplugged and completely cooled down before cleaning.

2. Remove Baskets and Accessories: Take out the baskets and any removable accessories, such as crisper plates or racks.

3. Wash Baskets and Accessories: Use warm, soapy water and a non-abrasive sponge to clean the baskets and accessories. These parts are also dishwasher-safe, making cleaning even more convenient. Refrain from using harsh detergents or scouring pads, as they can damage the non-stick coating.

4. Clean the Interior and Exterior: Wipe the interior of the air fryer with a damp cloth or sponge. Be careful not to allow water to seep into the heating element or electrical components. For the exterior, use a soft, damp cloth to remove any grease or food splatters.

5. Dry Thoroughly: Ensure all parts are completely dry before reassembling. This prevents rust and maintains the non-stick surface.

Deep Cleaning

1. Monthly Maintenance: Perform a deeper clean once a month or after cooking particularly greasy or odorous foods.

2. Remove Odours: To eliminate lingering smells, place a mixture of

Fundamentals of Ninja DoubleStack XL 2-Basket Air Fryer

water and lemon juice or vinegar in the baskets and run the air fryer at 180°C for 5-10 minutes. This will help neutralise any odours.

3. Check Heating Element: Gently wipe down the heating element with a damp cloth. Ensure it is completely dry before use.

4. Inspect for Wear and Tear: Regularly check for any signs of damage or wear. Replace any parts as necessary to maintain safety and efficiency.

General Tips

Avoid Abrasive Tools: Never use metal utensils or abrasive cleaning tools on any part of the air fryer, as they can scratch and damage the surfaces.
Store Properly: When not in use, store your air fryer in a cool, dry place to prevent dust accumulation and potential damage.

By following these cleaning and care instructions, your Ninja DoubleStack XL 2-Basket Air Fryer will continue to serve you well, delivering delicious and healthy meals for years to come.

Frequently Asked Questions & Notes

• **How do I adjust the time or temperature while using a single zone?**
Select the active zone, then press TEMP and use the dial to adjust the temperature or press TIME and use the dial to adjust the time.

• **How do I adjust the temperature or time while using dual zones?**
Select the desired zone, press TEMP and use the dial to adjust the temperature or press TIME and use the dial to adjust the time.

• **Does the unit need to pre-heat?**
The unit does not need to be pre-heated.

• **Can I cook different foods in each zone without worrying about cross-contamination?**
Yes, each zone is self-contained with its own heating elements and fans, preventing cross-contamination.

• **How do I pause the countdown?**
The countdown timer will pause automatically when you remove the baskets from the unit. Reinsert the basket within 15 minutes to resume cooking, or the zone with the basket open will be cancelled.

• **How do I pause one zone when using both zones?**
To pause one zone, first press the zone button, then press STOP/START. To pause both zones, simply press STOP/START.

• **Is the basket safe to put on my worktop?**
The basket will heat up during cooking. Use caution when handling and place it on heat-resistant surfaces only.

• **When should I use the crisper plate?**
Use the crisper plate when you want your food to come out crispy. The plate elevates the food in the basket, allowing air to flow underneath and around it, ensuring even cooking.

4-Week Meal Plan

Week 1

Day 1:
Breakfast: Soft Banana Bread
Lunch: Crunchy French Fries with Toum
Snack: Air-Fried Chicken Wings
Dinner: Buffalo Chicken Egg Rolls
Dessert: Almond-Baked Pears

Day 2:
Breakfast: Air-Fried Eggs
Lunch: Homemade Hush Puppies
Snack: Sweet & Spicy Walnuts
Dinner: Steamboat Shrimp and Tomato Salad
Dessert: Pecan-Stuffed Apple

Day 3:
Breakfast: Homemade Buttermilk Biscuits
Lunch: Roasted Cherry Tomatoes with Basil
Snack: Crunchy Kale Chips
Dinner: Beef-Rice Stuffed Peppers
Dessert: Dark Brownies

Day 4:
Breakfast: Garlic Butter Toast
Lunch: Air Fryer Mexican Street Corn
Snack: Crisp Apple Chips
Dinner: Juicy Teriyaki Chicken Legs
Dessert: Fluffy Chocolate Cake

Day 5:
Breakfast: Apple-Walnut Muffins
Lunch: Crisp Yuca Fries
Snack: Cheese Corn Dip
Dinner: Crispy Fish Sticks
Dessert: Homemade Custard

Day 6:
Breakfast: Classic Scotch Eggs
Lunch: Crunchy Potato Fries
Snack: Cheese Sausage Pizzas
Dinner: Classic Natchitoches Meat Pie
Dessert: Apple Hand Pies

Day 7:
Breakfast: Home-Fried Potatoes and Peppers
Lunch: Falafel with Cucumber-Tomato Salad
Snack: Crispy Corn Tortilla Chips
Dinner: Lamb Kofta with Tzatziki
Dessert: Crunch S'mores

Week 2

Day 1:
Breakfast: Crisp Bacon
Lunch: Spiced Carrots
Snack: Buffalo Chicken Bites
Dinner: Buttermilk-Fried Chicken Drumsticks
Dessert: Pumpkin Fritters

Day 2:
Breakfast: Nutty Whole Wheat Muffins
Lunch: Yummy Sweet Potato Fries
Snack: Sweet & Spicy Chicken Wings
Dinner: Salty and Sweet Salmon
Dessert: Chocolate-Frosted Doughnuts

Day 3:
Breakfast: Blueberry Pancake Poppers
Lunch: Corn on the Cob
Snack: BBQ Chicken Wings
Dinner: Sonoran Style Hot Dogs
Dessert: Chocolate Chip Cookies

Day 4:
Breakfast: Air-Fried Eggs
Lunch: Herbed Polenta Fries
Snack: Air-Fried Chicken Wings
Dinner: Crunchy Chicken Chunks
Dessert: Almond-Baked Pears

Day 5:
Breakfast: Homemade Buttermilk Biscuits
Lunch: Herb-Stuffed Potatoes
Snack: Sweet & Spicy Walnuts
Dinner: Coriander-Lime Shrimp
Dessert: Dark Brownies

Day 6:
Breakfast: Soft Banana Bread
Lunch: Crispy Brussels Sprouts with Mustard Aioli
Snack: Crunchy Kale Chips
Dinner: Teriyaki Baby Back Ribs
Dessert: Pecan-Stuffed Apple

Day 7:
Breakfast: Garlic Butter Toast
Lunch: Garlic Green Beans
Snack: Crisp Apple Chips
Dinner: Cumin Pork Tenderloin and Potatoes
Dessert: Fluffy Chocolate Cake

Week 3

Day 1:
Breakfast: Apple-Walnut Muffins
Lunch: Cheese-Bacon Stuffed Potatoes
Snack: Cheese Corn Dip
Dinner: Turkey-Hummus Cheese Wraps
Dessert: Homemade Custard

Day 2:
Breakfast: Classic Scotch Eggs
Lunch: Homemade Hush Puppies
Snack: Cheese Sausage Pizzas
Dinner: Savoury Salmon Croquettes
Dessert: Apple Hand Pies

Day 3:
Breakfast: Home-Fried Potatoes and Peppers
Lunch: Air Fryer Mexican Street Corn
Snack: Crispy Corn Tortilla Chips
Dinner: Authentic Carne Asada
Dessert: Crunch S'mores

Day 4:
Breakfast: Crisp Bacon
Lunch: Crunchy French Fries with Toum
Snack: Buffalo Chicken Bites
Dinner: Crispy Chicken Cutlets with Spaghetti
Dessert: Pumpkin Fritters

Day 5:
Breakfast: Blueberry Pancake Poppers
Lunch: Roasted Cherry Tomatoes with Basil
Snack: Sweet & Spicy Chicken Wings
Dinner: Beer-Battered Cod and Chips
Dessert: Chocolate-Frosted Doughnuts

Day 6:
Breakfast: Air-Fried Eggs
Lunch: Falafel with Cucumber-Tomato Salad
Snack: Sweet & Spicy Walnuts
Dinner: Bulgogi Burgers with Gochujang Mayonnaise
Dessert: Chocolate Chip Cookies

Day 7:
Breakfast: Soft Banana Bread
Lunch: Crisp Yuca Fries
Snack: BBQ Chicken Wings
Dinner: Spicy Pork Bulgogi
Dessert: Almond-Baked Pears

Week 4

Day 1:
Breakfast: Homemade Buttermilk Biscuits
Lunch: Crunchy Potato Fries
Snack: Crunchy Kale Chips
Dinner: Crunchy Chicken and Ranch Tortillas
Dessert: Pecan-Stuffed Apple

Day 2:
Breakfast: Nutty Whole Wheat Muffins
Lunch: Spiced Carrots
Snack: Cheese Corn Dip
Dinner: Delicious Firecracker Shrimp
Dessert: Dark Brownies

Day 3:
Breakfast: Garlic Butter Toast
Lunch: Yummy Sweet Potato Fries
Snack: Crisp Apple Chips
Dinner: Italian Cheese Sausage Meatballs
Dessert: Homemade Custard

Day 4:
Breakfast: Classic Scotch Eggs
Lunch: Corn on the Cob
Snack: Crispy Corn Tortilla Chips
Dinner: Spinach and Cream Cheese Stuffed Chicken
Dessert: Fluffy Chocolate Cake

Day 5:
Breakfast: Home-Fried Potatoes and Peppers
Lunch: Herb-Stuffed Potatoes
Snack: Cheese Sausage Pizzas
Dinner: Flavourful Kofta Kebabs
Dessert: Apple Hand Pies

Day 6:
Breakfast: Crisp Bacon
Lunch: Crispy Brussels Sprouts with Mustard Aioli
Snack: Buffalo Chicken Bites
Dinner: Spicy Cajun Shrimp
Dessert: Crunch S'mores

Day 7:
Breakfast: Blueberry Pancake Poppers
Lunch: Garlic Green Beans
Snack: Sweet & Spicy Chicken Wings
Dinner: Mint Lamb Kebabs
Dessert: Pumpkin Fritters

Chapter 1 Breakfast

Air-Fried Eggs 12

Soft Banana Bread 12

Homemade Buttermilk Biscuits 13

Garlic Butter Toast 13

Crisp Bacon 14

Apple-Walnut Muffins 14

Classic Scotch Eggs 15

Nutty Whole Wheat Muffins 15

Home-Fried Potatoes and Peppers 16

Blueberry Pancake Poppers 16

Air-Fried Eggs

⏱ **Prep: 1 minute** 🍳 **Cook: 12 minutes** 📚 **Serves: 4**

Ingredients:
4 eggs

Preparation:
1. Insert a crisper plate in a basket, place eggs in the basket, then insert the basket in Zone 1. The unit will default to Zone 1. Turn the dial to select AIR FRY, set the temperature to 150°C, and set the time to 9 minutes. Press START/PAUSE to begin cooking. 2. Your timing may vary slightly, but your eggs should be soft-cooked, with solid whites and still slightly runny yolks. 3. Cook 1 minute more for a slightly firmer yolk. 4. Cook for 2 to 3 more minutes (for a total of 12 to 13 minutes) for hard-cooked eggs.

Soft Banana Bread

⏱ **Prep: 5 minutes** 🍳 **Cook: 20 minutes** 📚 **Serves: 6**

Ingredients:
cooking spray
125g white wheat flour
½ teaspoon baking powder
¼ teaspoon salt
¼ teaspoon baking soda
1 egg
75g mashed ripe banana
60g plain yoghurt
60ml pure maple syrup
2 tablespoons coconut oil
½ teaspoon pure vanilla extract

Preparation:
1. Lightly spray a round baking dish with cooking spray. 2. In a medium bowl, mix together the flour, baking powder, salt, and soda. 3. In a separate bowl, beat the egg and add the mashed banana, yoghurt, syrup, oil, and vanilla. Mix until well combined. 4. Pour the liquid mixture into the dry ingredients and stir gently to blend. Do not beat. The batter may be slightly lumpy. 5. Pour the batter into the baking dish. 6. Insert a crisper plate in a basket, place the baking dish in the basket, then insert the basket in Zone 1. The unit will default to Zone 1. Turn the dial to select AIR FRY, set the temperature to 165°C, and set the time to 20 minutes. Press START/PAUSE to begin cooking. Cook until a toothpick inserted in the centre of the loaf comes out clean.

| Chapter 1 Breakfast

Homemade Buttermilk Biscuits

⏱ Prep: 10 minutes   🍲 Cook: 10 minutes   ❖ Serves: 4

Ingredients:

125g flour
1½ teaspoons baking powder
¼ teaspoon baking soda
¼ teaspoon salt
55g butter, cut into tiny cubes
60ml buttermilk, plus 2 tablespoons
cooking spray

Preparation:

1. Combine flour, baking powder, soda, and salt in a medium bowl. Stir together. 2. Add cubed butter and cut into flour using knives or a pastry blender. 3. Add buttermilk and stir into a stiff dough. 4. Divide the dough into 4 portions and shape each into a large biscuit. If the dough is too sticky to handle, stir in 1 or 2 more tablespoons of flour before shaping. Biscuits should be firm enough to hold their shape otherwise they will stick to the air fryer basket. 5. Insert the crisper plates in the baskets. Spray the crisper plates with nonstick cooking spray. 6. Divide the biscuits evenly between both baskets, then insert the baskets in the unit. The unit will default to Zone 1. Turn the dial to select AIR FRY. Set the temperature to 165°C and set the time to 10 minutes. Press the MATCH COOK button to copy Zone 1's settings to Zone 2. Press START/ PAUSE to begin cooking in both zones. 7. When cooking is complete, the unit will beep.

Garlic Butter Toast

⏱ Prep: 10 minutes   🍲 Cook: 5 minutes   ❖ Serves: 4

Ingredients:

55g butter
½ teaspoon lemon juice
½ clove garlic
½ teaspoon dried parsley flakes
4 slices Italian bread, 1-inch thick

Preparation:

1. Place butter, lemon juice, garlic, and parsley in a food processor. Process about 1 minute, or until garlic is pulverized and ingredients are well blended. 2. Spread garlic butter on both sides of bread slices. 3. Insert the crisper plates in the baskets. Place bread slices upright in both baskets, then insert the baskets in the unit. 4. The unit will default to Zone 1. Turn the dial to select AIR FRY. Set the temperature to 200°C and set the time to 5 minutes. Press the MATCH COOK button to copy Zone 1's settings to Zone 2. Press START/ PAUSE to begin cooking in both zones. 5. When cooking is complete, the unit will beep.

Chapter 1 Breakfast | 13

Crisp Bacon

⏱ **Prep: 5 minutes**   🍳 **Cook: 10 minutes**   📚 **Serves: 5**

Ingredients:
10 slices bacon

Preparation:
1. Cut the bacon slices in half, so they will fit in the air fryer. 2. Insert a crisper plate in the Zone 1 basket, place the half-slices in the basket in a single layer, then place one Stacked Meal Rack in the basket over the bacon. Place the remaining bacon on the rack, then insert the basket in Zone 1. 3. Select DOUBLE STACK PRO. Select Zone 1. Turn the dial to select AIR FRY, set the temperature to 200°C, and set the time to 5 minutes. Press START/PAUSE to begin cooking. 4. Check the bacon, reset the timer and fry for 5 minutes more. 5. When the time has elapsed, check the bacon again. If you like your bacon crispier, cook it for another 1 to 2 minutes.

Apple-Walnut Muffins

⏱ **Prep: 15 minutes**   🍳 **Cook: 10 minutes**   📚 **Serves: 8**

Ingredients:
125g flour
60g sugar
1 teaspoon baking powder
¼ teaspoon baking soda
¼ teaspoon salt
1 teaspoon cinnamon
¼ teaspoon ginger
¼ teaspoon nutmeg
1 egg
2 tablespoons pancake syrup, plus 2 teaspoons
2 tablespoons melted butter, plus 2 teaspoons
190g unsweetened applesauce
½ teaspoon vanilla extract
30g chopped walnuts
25g diced apple
8 foil muffin cups, liners removed and sprayed with cooking spray

Preparation:
1. In a large bowl, stir together flour, sugar, baking powder, baking soda, salt, cinnamon, ginger, and nutmeg. 2. In a small bowl, beat the egg until frothy. Add syrup, butter, applesauce, and vanilla and mix well. 3. Pour egg mixture into dry ingredients and stir just until moistened. 4. Gently stir in nuts and diced apple. 5. Divide batter among the 8 muffin cups. 6. Insert the crisper plates in the baskets. Place 4 muffin cups in each basket, then insert the baskets in the unit. The unit will default to Zone 1. Turn the dial to select AIR FRY. Set the temperature to 165°C and set the time to 10 minutes. Press the MATCH COOK button to copy Zone 1's settings to Zone 2. Press START/ PAUSE to begin cooking in both zones. Cook until the toothpick inserted in the centre comes out clean.

Chapter 1 Breakfast

Classic Scotch Eggs

⏰ **Prep: 10 minutes**　🍲 **Cook: 20 minutes**　🍃 **Serves: 4**

Ingredients:

2 tablespoons flour, plus extra for coating
455g ground breakfast sausage
4 hardboiled eggs, peeled
1 raw egg
1 tablespoon water
Oil for misting or cooking spray
Crumb Coating
65g panko breadcrumbs
95g flour

Preparation:

1. Combine flour with ground sausage and mix thoroughly. 2. Divide into 4 equal portions and mould each around a hardboiled egg so the sausage completely covers the egg. 3. In a small bowl, beat together the raw egg and water. 4. Dip sausage-covered eggs in the remaining flour, then the egg mixture, then roll in the crumb coating. 5. Insert a crisper plate in a basket, place the eggs in the basket, then insert the basket in Zone 1. The unit will default to Zone 1. Turn the dial to select AIR FRY, set the temperature to 180°C, and set the time to 10 minutes. Press START/PAUSE to begin cooking. 6. Continue cooking for 10 to 15 minutes more or until the sausage is well done.

Nutty Whole Wheat Muffins

⏰ **Prep: 15 minutes**　🍲 **Cook: 10 minutes**　🍃 **Serves: 8**

Ingredients:

60g whole-wheat flour, plus 2 tablespoons
25g oat bran
2 tablespoons flaxseed meal
45g brown sugar
½ teaspoon baking soda
½ teaspoon baking powder
¼ teaspoon salt
½ teaspoon cinnamon
120ml buttermilk
2 tablespoons melted butter
1 egg
½ teaspoon pure vanilla extract
55g grated carrots
25g chopped pecans
30g chopped walnuts
1 tablespoon pumpkin seeds
1 tablespoon sunflower seeds
16 foil muffin cups, paper liners removed
cooking spray

Preparation:

1. In a large bowl, stir together the flour, bran, flaxseed meal, sugar, baking soda, baking powder, salt, and cinnamon. 2. In a medium bowl, beat together the butter, egg, buttermilk, and vanilla. Pour into the flour mixture and stir just until dry ingredients moisten. Do not beat. 3. Gently stir in carrots, nuts, and seeds. 4. Double up the foil cups so you have 8 total and spray with cooking spray. 5. Insert the crisper plates in the baskets. Place 4 foil cups in each basket and divide the batter among them, then insert the baskets in the unit. 6. The unit will default to Zone 1. Turn the dial to select AIR FRY. Set the temperature to 165°C and set the time to 10 minutes. Press the MATCH COOK button to copy Zone 1's settings to Zone 2. Press START/ PAUSE to begin cooking in both zones. Cook until the toothpick inserted in the centre comes out clean.

Chapter 1 Breakfast

Home-Fried Potatoes and Peppers

⏱ Prep: 5 minutes   🍲 Cook: 25 minutes   ◆ Serves: 4

Ingredients:

3 large russet potatoes
1 tablespoon canola oil
1 tablespoon extra-virgin olive oil
1 teaspoon paprika
Salt
Pepper
160g chopped onion
110g chopped red bell pepper
110g chopped green bell pepper

Preparation:

1. Cut the potatoes into ½-inch cubes. Place them in a large bowl of cold water and let them soak for at least 30 minutes, ideally up to an hour. 2. After soaking, drain the potatoes and thoroughly dry them with paper towels before returning them to the empty bowl. 3. Add canola and olive oils, paprika, and salt and pepper to taste. Toss to fully coat the potatoes. 4. Insert a crisper plate in the Zone 1 basket, place half of the potatoes in the basket, then place one Stacked Meal Rack in the basket over the potatoes. Place the remaining potatoes on the rack, then insert the basket in Zone 1. 5. Select DOUBLE STACK PRO. Select Zone 1. Turn the dial to select AIR FRY, set the temperature to 185°C, and set the time to 20 minutes. Press START/PAUSE to begin cooking, shaking the air fryer basket every 5 minutes (a total of 4 times). 6. Add the onion and red and green bell peppers to the air fryer basket. Cook for an additional 3 to 4 minutes, or until the potatoes are cooked through and the peppers are soft. 7. Cool before serving.

Blueberry Pancake Poppers

⏱ Prep: 5 minutes   🍲 Cook: 8 minutes   ◆ Serves: 8

Ingredients:

125g all-purpose flour
1 tablespoon sugar
1 teaspoon baking soda
½ teaspoon baking powder
235ml milk
1 large egg
1 teaspoon vanilla extract
1 teaspoon olive oil
75g fresh blueberries

Preparation:

1. In a medium mixing bowl, combine the flour, sugar, baking soda, and baking powder and mix well. 2. Mix in the milk, egg, vanilla, and oil. 3. Coat the inside of an air fryer muffin tin with cooking spray. 4. Fill each muffin cup two-thirds full. 5. Drop a few blueberries into each muffin cup. 6. Insert a crisper plate in the Zone 1 basket, place half of the muffin cups in the basket, then place one Stacked Meal Rack in the basket over the muffin cups. Place the remaining muffin cups on the rack, then insert the basket in Zone 1. 7. Select DOUBLE STACK PRO. Select Zone 1. Turn the dial to select AIR FRY, set the temperature to 160°C, and set the time to 8 minutes. Press START/PAUSE to begin cooking. 8. Insert a toothpick into the centre of a pancake popper; if it comes out clean, they are done. If the batter clings to the toothpick, cook the poppers for 2 minutes more and check again. 9. When the poppers are cooked through, use silicone oven mitts to remove the muffin tin from the air fryer basket. Turn out the poppers onto a wire rack to cool.

Chapter 2 Vegetables and Sides

Herbed Polenta Fries …………………………………………………………………… 18

Homemade Hush Puppies …………………………………………………………… 18

Garlic Green Beans …………………………………………………………………… 19

Air Fryer Mexican Street Corn ……………………………………………………… 19

Roasted Cherry Tomatoes with Basil ……………………………………………… 20

Crisp Yuca Fries ………………………………………………………………………… 20

Crunchy Potato Fries ………………………………………………………………… 21

Spiced Carrots ………………………………………………………………………… 21

Yummy Sweet Potato Fries ………………………………………………………… 22

Herb-Stuffed Potatoes ……………………………………………………………… 22

Crispy Brussels Sprouts with Mustard Aioli ……………………………………… 23

Corn on the Cob ……………………………………………………………………… 23

Cheese-Bacon Stuffed Potatoes …………………………………………………… 24

Falafel with Cucumber-Tomato Salad …………………………………………… 25

Crunchy French Fries with Toum …………………………………………………… 26

Herbed Polenta Fries

⏱ Prep: 15 minutes 🍱 Cook: 24 minutes ❖ Serves: 4

Ingredients:

1 tube refrigerated polenta (about 510g)
1 tablespoon olive oil
½ teaspoon basil, crushed
¼ teaspoon oregano, crushed
¼ teaspoon garlic powder
Oil in mister
240g jarred Arrabbiata sauce, for dipping

Preparation:

1. Unwrap polenta and cut in half crosswise. Cut each half lengthwise into ½-inch sticks. Combine oil, basil, oregano, and garlic powder in a large bowl; add polenta sticks and toss. 2. Insert a crisper plate in the Zone 1 basket and spray with oil, place half of the polenta sticks in the basket, then place one Stacked Meal Rack in the basket over the polenta sticks. Place the remaining polenta sticks on the rack, then insert the basket in Zone 1. 3. Select DOUBLE STACK PRO. Select Zone 1. Turn the dial to select AIR FRY, set the temperature to 200°C, and set the time to 24 minutes. Press START/PAUSE to begin cooking. Shake the basket 3 times during cooking. (Fries will crisp after standing for a few minutes.) 4. Meanwhile, warm the sauce, covered, in a microwave on high for 90 seconds, or until heated through. Serve with polenta fries.

Homemade Hush Puppies

⏱ Prep: 10 minutes 🍱 Cook: 10 minutes ❖ Serves: 4

Ingredients:

140g cornmeal, preferably finely ground
65g all-purpose flour
1 tablespoon granulated sugar
1 teaspoon kosher salt
½ teaspoon baking soda
½ teaspoon black pepper
240ml buttermilk
2 tablespoons unsalted butter, melted
Vegetable oil for spraying

Preparation:

1. Whisk together the cornmeal, flour, sugar, salt, baking soda, and pepper in a medium bowl. Make a well in the centre of the dry ingredients. Pour in the buttermilk and melted butter and stir with a fork until the batter just comes together. Let the batter rest for 10 minutes. 2. Insert the crisper plates in the baskets. Using a small cookie scoop, scoop 5 or 6 circles of batter approximately 1½ inches (4 cm) in diameter directly onto each basket of the air fryer. Spray with oil, then insert the baskets in the unit. 3. The unit will default to Zone 1. Turn the dial to select AIR FRY. Set the temperature to 200°C and set the time to 10 minutes. Press the MATCH COOK button to copy Zone 1's settings to Zone 2. Press START/ PAUSE to begin cooking in both zones. 4. Cook until the outside is firm and browned and the inside is cooked through. Remove from the air fryer. Serve warm with butter.

Chapter 2 Vegetables and Sides

Garlic Green Beans

⏰ Prep: 5 minutes 🍲 Cook: 8 minutes ❖ Serves: 4

Ingredients:

680g green beans, trimmed
1 tablespoon extra-virgin olive oil
1 teaspoon garlic powder
Salt
Pepper

Preparation:

1. In a large bowl, drizzle the green beans with the olive oil. Sprinkle with the garlic powder and salt and pepper to taste. Mix well. 2. Insert a crisper plate in a basket, place the green beans in the basket, then insert the basket in Zone 1. The unit will default to Zone 1. Turn the dial to select AIR FRY, set the temperature to 200°C, and set the time to 4 minutes. Press START/PAUSE to begin cooking. 3. Shake the basket and cook for an additional 3 to 4 minutes, until the green beans have turned slightly brown. 4. Cool before serving.

Air Fryer Mexican Street Corn

⏰ Prep: 10 minutes 🍲 Cook: 10 minutes ❖ Serves: 4

Ingredients:

60ml Mexican crema
60g mayonnaise
1 lime
½ teaspoon garlic powder
Pinch cayenne pepper plus more for garnish
4 shucked ears of corn
2 tablespoons unsalted butter, melted
40g crumbled queso fresco (Mexican fresh cheese)
5g chopped coriander

Preparation:

1. Whisk together the crema, mayonnaise, the zest from the lime, the garlic powder, and a pinch of the cayenne pepper in a small bowl. Set aside. 2. Brush the ears of corn with the melted butter. 3. Insert a crisper plate in the Zone 1 basket, place 2 ears of corn in the basket, then place one Stacked Meal Rack in the basket over the corn. Place the remaining ears of corn on the rack, then insert the basket in Zone 1. 4. Select DOUBLE STACK PRO. Select Zone 1. Turn the dial to select AIR FRY, set the temperature to 200°C, and set the time to 10 minutes. Press START/PAUSE to begin cooking, rotating 2 or 3 times, until browned on all sides. Remove the ears of corn to a serving platter. 5. Brush the ears with the crema and mayonnaise mixture. Sprinkle the crumbled queso fresco and chopped coriander on top of the corn. Spritz the corn with the juice from the lime and sprinkle with additional cayenne pepper, if desired. Serve immediately.

Roasted Cherry Tomatoes with Basil

⏱ **Prep: 10 minutes**   🍴 **Cook: 30 minutes**   ≋ **Serves: 4**

Ingredients:

600g cherry or grape tomatoes
2 teaspoons extra-virgin olive oil
¼ teaspoon kosher salt
1 sprig basil

Preparation:

1. Toss the tomatoes with the olive oil and salt in a medium bowl. 2. Insert the crisper plates in the baskets. Divide the tomatoes evenly between both baskets, then insert the baskets in the unit. 3. The unit will default to Zone 1. Turn the dial to select ROAST. Set the temperature to 120°C and set the time to 30 minutes. Press the MATCH COOK button to copy Zone 1's settings to Zone 2. Press START/ PAUSE to begin cooking in both zones, shaking once or twice, until the tomatoes are softened and browned in places. Some tomatoes may have split or burst. Remove the tomatoes and place in a serving dish. 4. Remove the leaves from the sprig of basil and cut them into ribbons. Add the basil to the tomatoes. Serve warm or at room temperature.

Crisp Yuca Fries

⏱ **Prep: 10 minutes**   🍴 **Cook: 10 minutes**   ≋ **Serves: 4**

Ingredients:

3 yuca roots
Vegetable oil for spraying
1 teaspoon kosher salt

Preparation:

1. Trim the ends off the yuca roots and cut each one into 2 or 3 pieces depending on the length. Have a bowl of water ready. Peel off the rough outer skin with a paring knife or sharp vegetable peeler. Halve each piece of yuca lengthwise. Place the peeled pieces in a bowl of water to prevent them from oxidizing and turning brown. 2. Fill a large pot with water and bring to a boil over high heat. Season well with salt. Add the yuca pieces to the water and cook until they are tender enough to be pierced with a fork, but not falling apart, approximately 12 to 15 minutes. Drain. Some of the yuca pieces will have a fibrous string running down the centre. Remove it. Cut the yuca into 2 or 3 pieces to resemble thick-cut French fries. 3. Insert a crisper plate in the Zone 1 basket, place half of the yuca fries in a single layer in the basket, then place one Stacked Meal Rack in the basket over the yuca fries. Place the remaining yuca fries on the rack, then insert the basket in Zone 1. 4. Select DOUBLE STACK PRO. Select Zone 1. Turn the dial to select AIR FRY, set the temperature to 200°C, and set the time to 10 minutes. Press START/PAUSE to begin cooking, turning the fries halfway through, until the outside of the fries is crisp and browned and the inside fluffy. Spray the cooked yuca with oil and toss with 1 teaspoon salt. 5. Serve the yuca fries warm with toum, chipotle ketchup, or mint chimichurri.

20 | Chapter 2 Vegetables and Sides

Crunchy Potato Fries

⏰ Prep: 10 minutes   🍱 Cook: 20 minutes   ❖ Serves: 2

Ingredients:

1 large baking potato, peeled
2 tablespoons vegetable oil
½ teaspoon kosher salt
1 teaspoon black pepper
Gochujang Mayonnaise, for dipping

Preparation:

1. Cut the potato lengthwise into ¼-inch-thick slices. Lay each slice flat and cut lengthwise into fries about ¼ inch thick. 2. In a medium bowl, toss together the potatoes, salt, vegetable oil and pepper until well coated. 3. Insert a crisper plate in a basket, place the fries in a single layer in the basket, then insert the basket in Zone 1. (If they won't fit in a single layer, set a rack on top of the bottom layer of potatoes and place the rest of the potatoes on the rack. Select DOUBLE STACK PRO.) The unit will default to Zone 1. Turn the dial to select AIR FRY, set the temperature to 200°C, and set the time to 20 minutes. Press START/PAUSE to begin cooking, shaking halfway through the cooking time, until the fries are crisp and lightly browned. 4. Turn the fries out onto a serving platter. Serve immediately with gochujang mayonnaise for dipping.

Spiced Carrots

⏰ Prep: 15 minutes   🍱 Cook: 15 minutes   ❖ Serves: 4

Ingredients:

6 carrots (about 565g), peeled, halved crosswise and lengthwise
1 tablespoon olive oil
1 tablespoon packed fresh oregano leaves, chopped
½ teaspoon smoked paprika
¼ teaspoon ground nutmeg
¼ teaspoon salt
⅛ teaspoon pepper
1 tablespoon butter, melted
1 tablespoon red wine vinegar
2 tablespoons roasted, salted, shelled pistachios, chopped

Preparation:

1. Toss together carrots, oil, oregano, paprika, nutmeg, salt, and pepper. 2. Insert a crisper plate in a basket, place the carrots in the basket, then insert the basket in Zone 1. The unit will default to Zone 1. Turn the dial to select AIR FRY, set the temperature to 185°C, and set the time to 15 minutes. Press START/PAUSE to begin cooking, tossing a few times, until lightly browned and tender. 3. Transfer to a serving platter. Drizzle with butter and vinegar, and sprinkle with pistachios.

Yummy Sweet Potato Fries

⏰ Prep: 15 minutes   🍲 Cook: 22 minutes   ◆ Serves: 4

Ingredients:
455g sweet potatoes (1 large)
¾ teaspoon cornstarch
1½ teaspoons olive oil
¼ teaspoon salt
¾ teaspoon chilli powder (optional)

Preparation:
1. Cut sweet potatoes into ¼-inch-wide sticks. Soak in water for 10 minutes; drain well and pat dry. In a bowl, toss potatoes in cornstarch until evenly coated. 2. Insert a crisper plate in a basket, place the potatoes in the basket, then insert the basket in Zone 1. The unit will default to Zone 1. Turn the dial to select AIR FRY, set the temperature to 190°C, and set the time to 15 minutes. Press START/PAUSE to begin cooking, shaking once. 3. Return to bowl and toss with oil, ¼ teaspoon salt, and chilli powder, if using, until evenly coated. Reduce temperature to 150°C. Place in the basket and air-fry until tender and golden brown, 7 minutes.

Herb-Stuffed Potatoes

⏰ Prep: 50 minutes   🍲 Cook: 30 minutes   ◆ Serves: 6

Ingredients:
3 large russet potatoes (1245g), well-scrubbed
1 medium shallot
5g packed fresh basil leaves
4 tablespoons Parmesan cheese
2 tablespoons butter
¼ teaspoon dried marjoram
½ teaspoon salt
½ teaspoon freshly ground black pepper
2 tablespoons low-fat sour cream
80ml 2% milk

Preparation:
1. With a fork, pierce each potato 3 times; place on a sheet of parchment paper in the microwave. Microwave on High for 15 minutes, or until tender, turning once. Cover with a kitchen towel; let cool. 2. Meanwhile, finely chop shallots and basil. Grate Parmesan. 3. Combine butter and shallots in a small bowl; cover with plastic. Microwave on High for 1½ minutes, until shallots are softened. Place in a large bowl with marjoram, basil, 3 tablespoons Parmesan, salt, and pepper. 4. Cut potatoes crosswise in half. Trim off the rounded ends so that the potatoes stand upright. With a spoon, scoop out potato flesh, leaving ¼-inch shell; place the flesh in a bowl. Add sour cream and milk; mash well. Spoon mixture into shells. Top with remaining 1 tablespoon Parmesan. 5. Insert a crisper plate in a basket, place the potatoes in the basket, then insert the basket in Zone 1. The unit will default to Zone 1. Turn the dial to select AIR FRY, set the temperature to 190°C, and set the time to 12 minutes. Press START/PAUSE to begin cooking. Cook until golden brown and heated through.

Crispy Brussels Sprouts with Mustard Aioli

⏱ **Prep: 5 minutes**   🍳 **Cook: 12 minutes**   ≋ **Serves: 4**

Ingredients:

For the Brussels Sprouts:
455g Brussels sprouts, halved
1 teaspoon garlic powder
Salt
Pepper
Cooking oil

For the Mustard Aioli:
110g mayonnaise
½ tablespoon olive oil
1 tablespoon Dijon mustard
1 teaspoon minced garlic
Salt
Pepper
1 tablespoon chopped parsley

Preparation:

To make the Brussels sprouts: 1. In a large bowl, combine the Brussels sprouts with the garlic powder. Season with salt and pepper to taste. 2. Insert a crisper plate in a basket, place the Brussels sprouts in the basket, then insert the basket in Zone 1. The unit will default to Zone 1. Turn the dial to select AIR FRY, set the temperature to 195°C, and set the time to 6 minutes. Press START/PAUSE to begin cooking. 3. Shake the basket and cook for an additional 6 to 7 minutes, until the Brussels sprouts have turned slightly brown.

To make the mustard aioli: 1. While the Brussels sprouts are cooking, combine the mayonnaise, olive oil, mustard, and garlic in a small bowl, adding salt and black pepper to taste. Mix well until fully combined. Sprinkle with parsley to garnish. 2. Cool the Brussels sprouts and serve alongside the aioli.

Corn on the Cob

⏱ **Prep: 5 minutes**   🍳 **Cook: 12 minutes**   ≋ **Serves: 4**

Ingredients:

4 ears of corn on the cob, shucked

Preparation:

1. Insert the crisper plates in the baskets. Trim corn, if needed, to the fit air fryer and place in both baskets, then insert the baskets in the unit. 2. The unit will default to Zone 1. Turn the dial to select AIR FRY. Set the temperature to 190°C and set the time to 12 minutes. Press the MATCH COOK button to copy Zone 1's settings to Zone 2. Press START/ PAUSE to begin cooking in both zones, turning over with tongs halfway through.

Cheese-Bacon Stuffed Potatoes

Prep: 15 minutes **Cook: 42 minutes** **Serves: 8**

Ingredients:

4 large russet potatoes
4 slices bacon
2 tablespoons butter
120ml milk
1 teaspoon garlic powder
Salt
Pepper
2 scallions, green parts (white parts optional), chopped
2 tablespoons sour cream
120g shredded cheddar cheese, divided

Preparation:

1. Using a fork, poke three holes into the top of each potato. 2. Insert a crisper plate in a basket, place the potatoes in the basket, then insert the basket in Zone 1. The unit will default to Zone 1. Turn the dial to select AIR FRY, set the temperature to 200°C, and set the time to 40 minutes. Press START/PAUSE to begin cooking. 3. Meanwhile, in a skillet over medium-high heat, cook the bacon for about 5 to 7 minutes, flipping to evenly crisp. Drain on paper towels, crumble, and set aside. 4. Remove the cooked potatoes from the air fryer and allow them to cool for 10 minutes. 5. While the potatoes cool, heat a saucepan over medium-high heat. Add the butter and milk. Stir. Allow the mixture to cook for 2 to 3 minutes, until the butter has melted. 6. Halve each of the potatoes lengthwise. Scoop half of the flesh out of the middle of each potato half, leaving the flesh on the surrounding edges. This will hold the potato together when you stuff it. 7. Place the potato flesh in a large bowl and mash with a potato masher. Add the warm butter and milk mixture and stir to combine. Season with the garlic powder and salt and pepper to taste. 8. Add the cooked bacon, scallions, sour cream, and 4/5ths of cheddar cheese. Stir to combine. 9. Stuff each potato half with 1 to 2 tablespoons of the mashed potato mixture. Sprinkle the remaining cheddar cheese on top of the potato halves. 10. Insert the crisper plates in the baskets. Place 4 potato halves in each basket. Do not stack, then insert the baskets in the unit. The unit will default to Zone 1. Turn the dial to select AIR FRY. Set the temperature to 200°C and set the time to 2 minutes. Press the MATCH COOK button to copy Zone 1's settings to Zone 2. Press START/ PAUSE to begin cooking in both zones. 11. Remove the cooked potatoes from the air fryer. Cool before serving.

| Chapter 2 Vegetables and Sides

Falafel with Cucumber-Tomato Salad

⏱ **Prep: 25 minutes**   🍲 **Cook: 14 minutes**   ❖ **Serves: 4**

Ingredients:

1 lemon
5g fresh mint leaves
3 cloves garlic
1 teaspoon ground cumin
1 teaspoon ground coriander
60g packed flat-leaf parsley
1⅛ teaspoons salt
½ teaspoon pepper
2 425g cans chickpeas, rinsed and drained
3 tablespoons all-purpose flour
Oil in mister
80g tahini (sesame paste)
4 tablespoons extra-virgin olive oil
455g tomatoes, chopped
2 seedless (English) cucumbers, chopped
½ small red onion, finely chopped
Toasted pita bread, for serving

Preparation:

1. From lemon, grate 1 teaspoon peel and squeeze 3 tablespoons juice; set aside. 2. In a food processor bowl, place mint, garlic, cumin, coriander, lemon peel, half of the parsley, and ½ teaspoon each salt and pepper; pulse until finely chopped. Add chickpeas and flour; pulse until just chopped and well mixed, occasionally scraping down the side of the bowl with a rubber spatula. 3. With a measuring cup, scoop a scant ¼ of the mixture and shape into 12 (2-inch-diameter) patties. Spray the tops of the patties with oil. 4. Insert a crisper plate in the Zone 1 basket, place half of the patties, oil side down, in the basket; spray with oil. Then place one Stacked Meal Rack in the basket over the patties. Place the remaining patties on the rack, then insert the basket in Zone 1. 5. Select DOUBLE STACK PRO. Select Zone 1. Turn the dial to select AIR FRY, set the temperature to 200°C, and set the time to 14 minutes. Press START/PAUSE to begin cooking. Cook until golden brown. 6. Meanwhile, in a small bowl, whisk together tahini, 2 tablespoons olive oil, 120ml cold water, and ⅛ teaspoon salt until smooth; set aside. In a large bowl, toss tomatoes with cucumbers, onion, reserved lemon juice, remaining 30g parsley, remaining 2 tablespoons olive oil, and ½ teaspoon salt. 6. Serve falafel with salad; drizzle with tahini sauce. Serve with toasted pita.

Crunchy French Fries with Toum

⏰ **Prep: 10 minutes**   🍲 **Cook: 22 minutes**   ❖ **Serves: 4**

Ingredients:

910g russet potatoes, cut into ½-inch-thick (1.3 cm) fries
135g garlic cloves, peeled
3 teaspoons kosher salt, divided
5 to 6 tablespoons freshly squeezed lemon juice, chilled or iced, divided
600ml canola or other neutral oil, chilled, divided, plus 1 tablespoon

Preparation:

1. Place the potato fries in a large bowl and cover with cold water. Soak for at least 30 minutes and up to several hours to remove excess starch. 2. While the potatoes are soaking, make the toum. Place the garlic cloves in a food processor along with 2 teaspoons of the salt. Pulse several times, scraping down the sides of the bowl as necessary, until the garlic is finely minced. Add 1 tablespoon of lemon juice and pulse again until a paste forms. With the motor running, slowly add 120ml of the oil in a steady stream. Add an additional tablespoon of lemon juice and pulse. Then, with the motor running, slowly add a second 120ml of oil, followed by the third tablespoon of lemon juice. 3. Repeat this process until you have used all the oil. Transfer the toum, which should be fluffy and similar in texture to a mousse, to a serving bowl or container, if not using right away, and refrigerate until needed. 4. Drain the potatoes and pat dry. Toss with the remaining 1 tablespoon of oil and the remaining teaspoon of salt. 5. Insert a crisper plate in the Zone 1 basket, place half of the potato fries in the basket, then place one Stacked Meal Rack in the basket over the potatoes. Place the remaining potato fries on the rack, then insert the basket in Zone 1. 6. Select DOUBLE STACK PRO. Select Zone 1. Turn the dial to select AIR FRY, set the temperature to 190°C, and set the time to 22 minutes. Press START/PAUSE to begin cooking, shaking and turning every 5 minutes or so, until the potatoes are browned on all sides and crispy. You also can cook them in two zones. 7. Toss the potatoes with additional salt, if desired. Serve the steak fries immediately with toum for dipping.

Chapter 3 Snacks and Starters

Air-Fried Chicken Wings	28
Sweet & Spicy Walnuts	28
Crunchy Kale Chips	29
Crisp Apple Chips	29
Cheese Corn Dip	30
Cheese Sausage Pizzas	30
Crispy Corn Tortilla Chips	31
Buffalo Chicken Bites	31
Sweet & Spicy Chicken Wings	32
BBQ Chicken Wings	32

Air-Fried Chicken Wings

⏰ Prep: 10 minutes 🍲 Cook: 18 minutes ❖ Serves: 6

Ingredients:

910g chicken wings, tips removed
⅛ teaspoon salt

Preparation:

1. Season the wings with salt. 2. Insert a crisper plate in the Zone 1 basket, place half of the chicken wings in the basket, then place one Stacked Meal Rack in the basket over the chicken wings. Place the remaining chicken wings on the rack, then insert the basket in Zone 1. 3. Select DOUBLE STACK PRO. Select Zone 1. Turn the dial to select AIR FRY, set the temperature to 200°C, and set the time to 18 minutes. Press START/PAUSE to begin cooking, turning the wings with tongs halfway through cooking. Transfer to a large bowl and toss with sauce until evenly coated. 4. Serve immediately.

Sweet & Spicy Walnuts

⏰ Prep: 10 minutes 🍲 Cook: 22 minutes ❖ Serves: 8

Ingredients:

95g sugar
1 teaspoon salt
½ teaspoon ground cinnamon
½ teaspoon ground cumin
½ teaspoon black pepper
¼ teaspoon ground red pepper (cayenne)
1 large egg white
360g unsalted walnuts (or mixed nuts)
Oil in mister

Preparation:

1. In a small bowl, combine sugar, salt, cinnamon, cumin, black pepper, and red pepper; stir until blended. In a large bowl, with a wire whisk, beat egg white until foamy. Measure 1 tablespoon of the beaten egg white and set aside for another use or discard; keep the rest. Add nuts to egg white in the large bowl; stir to coat evenly. Add sugar mixture; toss until nuts are thoroughly coated. 2. Insert the crisper plates in the baskets and spray with oil. Divide the nut mixture evenly between both baskets, then insert the baskets in the unit. The unit will default to Zone 1. Turn the dial to select AIR FRY. Set the temperature to 150°C and set the time to 22 minutes. Press the MATCH COOK button to copy Zone 1's settings to Zone 2. Press START/ PAUSE to begin cooking in both zones. Cook until nuts are golden brown and dry, stirring nuts from bottom to top with a spatula a few times. Spread the nuts out on the baking sheet and let them cool completely. 3. Store in an airtight container at room temperature for up to 1 month.

Crunchy Kale Chips

⏰ **Prep: 15 minutes**   🍴 **Cook: 8 minutes**   🍃 **Serves: 5**

Ingredients:

170g de-ribbed kale leaves, torn into 2-inch pieces
1½ tablespoons olive oil
¾ teaspoon chilli powder
½ teaspoon paprika
¼ teaspoon garlic powder
2 teaspoons sesame seeds

Preparation:

1. Toss together kale, oil, chilli powder, paprika, garlic powder, and sesame seeds. Massage kale for 1 minute. 2. Insert a crisper plate in a basket, place kale in the basket, then insert the basket in Zone 1. The unit will default to Zone 1. Turn the dial to select AIR FRY, set the temperature to 175°C, and set the time to 8 minutes. Press START/PAUSE to begin cooking, turning kale twice with tongs. 3. Cool and store in an airtight container for up to 1 week.

Crisp Apple Chips

⏰ **Prep: 5 minutes**   🍴 **Cook: 25 minutes**   🍃 **Serve: 1**

Ingredients:

1 Honeycrisp or pink lady apple

Preparation:

1. Core the apple with an apple corer, leaving the apple whole. Cut apple into ⅛-inch-thick slices. 2. Insert a crisper plate in a basket, arrange apple slices in the basket, staggering slices as much as possible. Then insert the basket in Zone 1. The unit will default to Zone 1. Turn the dial to select AIR FRY, set the temperature to 150°C, and set the time to 25 minutes. Press START/PAUSE to begin cooking. Cook until chips are dry and some are lightly browned, turning 4 times with tongs to separate and rotate them from top to bottom. 3. Place the chips in a single layer on a wire rack to cool. Apples will become crisper as they cool.

Cheese Corn Dip

⏱ **Prep: 15 minutes** 🍳 **Cook: 37 minutes** 🍽 **Serves: 8**

Ingredients:

115g cream cheese, softened
60g nonfat Greek yoghurt
60ml low-fat milk
3 tablespoons mayonnaise
1 chipotle in adobo sauce, finely chopped (1 tablespoon)
¼ teaspoon garlic powder
80g frozen corn, thawed
95g shredded Mexican cheese blend, divided
2 tablespoons chopped fresh coriander leaves
Air-Fried Tortilla Chips (recipe right), for serving

Preparation:

1. Beat cream cheese until smooth. Beat in yoghurt, milk, mayonnaise, chipotle, and garlic powder until blended. Add corn and ¾ of the cheese; beat for 1 minute on medium speed. Pour into a baking dish that fits the air fryer basket. Cover the dish tightly with foil. 2. Insert a crisper plate in a basket. Make a sling out of foil. Place the dish on the sling and put it in the basket, then insert the basket in Zone 1. The unit will default to Zone 1. Turn the dial to select AIR FRY, set the temperature to 195°C, and set the time to 30 minutes. Press START/PAUSE to begin cooking. 3. Uncover and air-fry for 5 more minutes, or until the dip is bubbly at the edges. Sprinkle with the remaining cheese and air-fry for 2 more minutes, or until the cheese melts. 4. Top with coriander and serve warm with tortilla chips.

Cheese Sausage Pizzas

⏱ **Prep: 10 minutes** 🍳 **Cook: 5 minutes** 🍽 **Serves: 4**

Ingredients:

55g pizza dough
2 tablespoons marinara sauce
55g provolone cheese, torn into pieces
2 links breakfast sausage, thinly sliced
1 bunch fresh parsley, chopped (for serving)

Preparation:

1. Separate the dough into 4 balls and roll out each ball on a lightly floured surface. 2. Top each pizza with equal amounts of marinara sauce, provolone cheese, and sausage. 3. Insert the crisper plates in the baskets and spray them with nonstick cooking spray, then place 2 pizzas in each basket. Place a Stacked Meal Rack in each basket over the pizza. Place the remaining 2 pizzas on the rack, then insert the basket in Zone 1. Select DOUBLE STACK PRO. Select Zone 1. Turn the dial to select AIR FRY, set the temperature to 180°C, and set the time to 5 minutes. Press the MATCH COOK button to copy Zone 1's settings to Zone 2. Press START/PAUSE to begin cooking in both zones. 4. Remove the pizzas from the fryer, sprinkle the parsley on top, and allow to cool on a wire rack for 5 minutes before serving.

Chapter 3 Snacks and Starters

Crispy Corn Tortilla Chips

⏲ **Prep: 10 minutes** 🍲 **Cook: 4 minutes** ❖ **Serves: 4**

Ingredients:

4 six-inch corn tortillas
1 tablespoon canola oil
¼ teaspoon kosher salt

Preparation:

1. Stack the corn tortillas, cut in half, then slice into thirds. 2. Insert a crisper plate in a basket and spray with nonstick cooking spray, then brush the tortillas with canola oil and place in the basket. Then insert the basket in Zone 1. The unit will default to Zone 1. Turn the dial to select AIR FRY, set the temperature to 180°C, and set the time to 4 minutes. Press START/PAUSE to begin cooking. Cook until golden brown and crispy. 3. Remove the chips from the fryer and place on a plate lined with a paper towel. Sprinkle the kosher salt on top before serving warm.

Buffalo Chicken Bites

⏲ **Prep: 10 minutes** 🍲 **Cook: 11 minutes** ❖ **Serves: 4**

Ingredients:

225g boneless and skinless chicken thighs, cut into 30 pieces
¼ teaspoon kosher salt
2 tablespoons hot sauce

Preparation:

1. Season the chicken bites with the kosher salt. 2. Insert a crisper plate in a basket and spray with nonstick cooking spray. Place the chicken bites in the basket, then insert the basket in Zone 1. The unit will default to Zone 1. Turn the dial to select AIR FRY, set the temperature to 200°C, and set the time to 11 minutes. Press START/PAUSE to begin cooking. 3. While the chicken bites cook, pour the hot sauce into a large bowl. 4. Remove the bites from the fryer and add to the sauce bowl, tossing to coat. Serve warm.

Sweet & Spicy Chicken Wings

⏰ Prep: 10 minutes　🍲 Cook: 15 minutes　📚 Serves: 4

Ingredients:

1 tablespoon Sriracha hot sauce
1 tablespoon honey
1 garlic clove, minced
½ teaspoon kosher salt
16 chicken wings and drumettes

Preparation:

1. In a large bowl, whisk together the Sriracha hot sauce, minced garlic, honey, and kosher salt, then add the chicken and toss to coat. 2. Insert a crisper plate in the Zone 1 basket and spray with nonstick cooking spray, place half of the wings in the basket, then place one Stacked Meal Rack in the basket over the wings. Place the remaining wings on the rack, then insert the basket in the unit. 3. Select DOUBLE STACK PRO. Select Zone 1. Turn the dial to select AIR FRY, set the temperature to 180°C, and set the time to 15 minutes. Press START/PAUSE to begin cooking, turning halfway through. 4. Remove the wings from the fryer and allow to cool on a wire rack for 10 minutes before serving.

BBQ Chicken Wings

⏰ Prep: 10 minutes　🍲 Cook: 2 minutes　📚 Serves: 4

Ingredients:

60g BBQ sauce
1 teaspoon balsamic vinegar
1 batch Chicken wings

Preparation:

1. In a small bowl, whisk together the BBQ sauce and vinegar, then use a brush to coat the Chicken Fingers with an even layer of sauce. 2. Insert a crisper plate in the Zone 1 basket and spray with nonstick cooking spray, place half of the wings in the basket, then place one Stacked Meal Rack in the basket over the wings. Place the remaining wings on the rack, then insert the basket in the unit. 3. Select DOUBLE STACK PRO. Select Zone 1. Turn the dial to select AIR FRY, set the temperature to 150°C, and set the time to 2 minutes. Press START/PAUSE to begin cooking. 4. Remove the wings from the fryer and place on a serving plate. Serve warm.

Chapter 4 Poultry

Juicy Teriyaki Chicken Legs …………………………………………………………… 34

Buffalo Chicken Egg Rolls …………………………………………………………… 34

Crunchy Chicken Chunks …………………………………………………………… 35

Buttermilk-Fried Chicken Drumsticks …………………………………………………………… 35

Turkey-Hummus Cheese Wraps …………………………………………………………… 36

Crispy Chicken Cutlets with Spaghetti …………………………………………………………… 36

Air Fryer Chicken Drumsticks with Honey BBQ Sauce …………………………………………………………… 37

Crunchy Chicken and Ranch Tortillas …………………………………………………………… 37

Garlicky Chicken Wings …………………………………………………………… 38

Spinach and Cream Cheese Stuffed Chicken …………………………………………………………… 38

Juicy Teriyaki Chicken Legs

⏲ Prep: 12 minutes   🍱 Cook: 20 minutes   ≋ Serves: 2

Ingredients:

4 tablespoons teriyaki sauce
1 tablespoon orange juice
1 teaspoon smoked paprika
4 chicken legs
1 chopped green onion
2 teaspoons sesame seeds
cooking spray

Preparation:

1. Mix together the teriyaki sauce, orange juice, and smoked paprika. Brush on all sides of the chicken legs. 2. Insert a crisper plate in a basket and spray with nonstick cooking spray, place the chicken in the basket, then insert the basket in Zone 1. The unit will default to Zone 1. Turn the dial to select AIR FRY, set the temperature to 180°C, and set the time to 6 minutes. Press START/PAUSE to begin cooking. 3. Turn and baste with sauce. Cook for 6 more minutes, turn and baste. Cook for 6 to 8 minutes more, until juices run clear when the chicken is pierced with a fork. 4. Sprinkle with chopped green onion and sesame seeds.

Buffalo Chicken Egg Rolls

⏲ Prep: 20 minutes   🍱 Cook: 9 minutes   ≋ Serves: 8

Ingredients:

1 teaspoon water
1 tablespoon cornstarch
1 egg
615g cooked chicken, diced or shredded
55g chopped green onion
40g diced celery
90g buffalo wing sauce
8 egg roll wraps
oil for misting or cooking spray
Blue Cheese Dip:
85g cream cheese, softened
80g blue cheese, crumbled
1 teaspoon Worcestershire sauce
¼ teaspoon garlic powder
60ml buttermilk (or sour cream)

Preparation:

1. Mix water and cornstarch in a small bowl until dissolved. Add egg, beat well, and set aside. 2. In a medium bowl, mix together chicken, green onion, celery, and buffalo wing sauce. 3. Divide chicken mixture evenly among 8 egg roll wraps, spooning ½ inch from one edge. 4. Moisten all edges of each wrap with beaten egg wash. 5. Fold the short ends over the filling, then roll up tightly and press to seal the edges. 6. Brush the outside of the wraps with egg wash, then spritz with oil or cooking spray. 7. Insert a crisper plate in the Zone 1 basket, place 4 egg rolls in the basket, then place one Stacked Meal Rack in the basket over the egg rolls. Place the remaining egg rolls on the rack, then insert the basket in the unit. 8. Select DOUBLE STACK PRO. Select Zone 1. Turn the dial to select AIR FRY, set the temperature to 200°C, and set the time to 9 minutes. Press START/PAUSE to begin cooking. Cook until the outside is brown and crispy. 9. While the rolls are cooking, prepare the Blue Cheese Dip. With a fork, mash together cream cheese and blue cheese. 10. Stir in the remaining ingredients. 11. The dip should be just thick enough to slightly cling to the egg rolls. If too thick, stir in buttermilk or milk, 1 tablespoon at a time until it reaches your desired consistency. 12. Serve while hot with Blue Cheese Dip, more buffalo wing sauce, or both.

| Chapter 4 Poultry

Crunchy Chicken Chunks

⏰ **Prep: 10 minutes** 🍲 **Cook: 10 minutes** ❖ **Serves: 4**

Ingredients:

455g chicken tenders cut in large chunks, about 1½ inches
salt and pepper
65g cornstarch
2 eggs, beaten
85g panko breadcrumbs
oil for misting or cooking spray

Preparation:

1. Season chicken chunks to your liking with salt and pepper. 2. Dip chicken chunks in cornstarch. Then dip in egg and shake off excess. Then roll in panko crumbs to coat well. 3. Spray all sides of chicken chunks with oil or cooking spray. 4. Insert a crisper plate in a basket, place the chicken in the basket, then insert the basket in Zone 1. The unit will default to Zone 1. Turn the dial to select AIR FRY, set the temperature to 200°C, and set the time to 5 minutes. Press START/PAUSE to begin cooking. Spray with oil, turn chunks over, and spray the other side. 5. Cook for an additional 3 to 5 minutes or until chicken juices run clear and outside is golden brown.

Buttermilk-Fried Chicken Drumsticks

⏰ **Prep: 10 minutes** 🍲 **Cook: 25 minutes** ❖ **Serves: 2**

Ingredients:

1 egg
120ml buttermilk
95g self-rising flour
65g seasoned panko breadcrumbs
1 teaspoon salt
¼ teaspoon ground black pepper (to mix into coating)
4 chicken drumsticks, skin on
oil for misting or cooking spray

Preparation:

1. Beat together the egg and buttermilk in a shallow bowl. 2. In a second shallow bowl, combine the flour, panko crumbs, salt, and pepper. 3. Sprinkle chicken drumsticks with additional salt and pepper to taste. 4. Dip the chicken drumsticks in the buttermilk mixture, then roll in the panko mixture, pressing in the crumbs to make the coating stick. Mist with oil or cooking spray. 5. Insert a crisper plate in a basket and spray with cooking spray. Place the chicken drumsticks in the basket, then insert the basket in Zone 1. The unit will default to Zone 1. Turn the dial to select AIR FRY, set the temperature to 180°C, and set the time to 20 minutes. Press START/PAUSE to begin cooking. Flip them halfway through cooking time. 6. Turn pieces to check for browning. If you have any white spots that haven't begun to brown, spritz them with oil or cooking spray. Continue cooking for an additional 5 minutes or until the crust is golden brown and the juices run clear. Larger, meatier drumsticks will take longer to cook than small ones.

Turkey-Hummus Cheese Wraps

⏲ **Prep: 10 minutes** 🍲 **Cook: 6 minutes** 🍽 **Serves: 4**

Ingredients:

4 large whole wheat wraps
125g hummus
16 thin slices deli turkey
8 slices provolone cheese
30g fresh baby spinach (or more to taste)

Preparation:

1. To assemble, place 2 tablespoons of hummus on each wrap and spread to within about a half inch from the edges. Top with 4 slices of turkey and 2 slices of provolone. Finish with ¼ of the baby spinach—or pile on as much as you like. 2. Roll up each wrap. You don't need to fold or seal the ends. 3. Insert a crisper plate in the Zone 1 basket, place 2 wraps in the basket, seam side down. Then place one Stacked Meal Rack in the basket over the wraps. Place the remaining wraps on the rack, then insert the basket in the unit. 4. Select DOUBLE STACK PRO. Select Zone 1. Turn the dial to select AIR FRY, set the temperature to 180°C, and set the time to 4 minutes. Press START/PAUSE to begin cooking. 5. If you like, you can continue cooking for 2 or 3 more minutes, until the wrap is slightly crispy.

Crispy Chicken Cutlets with Spaghetti

⏲ **Prep: 15 minutes** 🍲 **Cook: 10 minutes** 🍽 **Serves: 4**

Ingredients:

4 chicken tenders
Italian seasoning
salt
30g cornstarch
120ml Italian salad dressing
20g panko breadcrumbs
25g grated Parmesan cheese, plus more for serving
oil for misting or cooking spray
225g spaghetti, cooked
1 jar (680g) marinara sauce

Preparation:

1. Pound chicken tenders with a meat mallet or rolling pin until about ¼-inch thick. 2. Sprinkle both sides with Italian seasoning and salt to taste. 3. Place the cornstarch and salad dressing in 2 separate shallow dishes. 4. In a third shallow dish, mix together the panko crumbs and Parmesan cheese. 5. Dip flattened chicken in cornstarch, then salad dressing. Dip in the panko mixture, pressing into the chicken so the coating sticks well. 6. Spray both sides with oil or cooking spray. Insert a crisper plate in the Zone 1 basket, place 2 chicken tenders in the basket, then place one Stacked Meal Rack in the basket over the chicken tenders. Place the remaining chicken tenders on the rack, then insert the basket in the unit. 7. Select DOUBLE STACK PRO. Select Zone 1. Turn the dial to select AIR FRY, set the temperature to 200°C, and set the time to 5 minutes. Press START/PAUSE to begin cooking. Spray with oil again, turning the chicken to coat both sides. 8. Cook for an additional 4 to 6 minutes or until chicken juices run clear and the outside is browned. 9. While chicken is cooking, heat marinara sauce and stir into cooked spaghetti. 10. To serve, divide spaghetti with sauce among 4 dinner plates, and top each with a fried chicken tender. Pass additional Parmesan at the table for those who want extra cheese.

Chapter 4 Poultry

Air Fryer Chicken Drumsticks with Honey BBQ Sauce

Prep: 5 minutes   **Cook: 18 minutes**   **Serves: 5**

Ingredients:

10 chicken drumsticks
Chicken seasoning or rub
Salt
Pepper
Cooking oil
85g honey
250g barbecue sauce

Preparation:

1. Season the drumsticks with chicken seasoning, salt, and pepper to taste. 2. Insert a crisper plate in the Zone 1 basket and spray with cooking oil, place the drumsticks in one layer in the basket, then place one Stacked Meal Rack in the basket over the drumsticks. Place the remaining drumsticks on the rack and spray the chicken with cooking oil. Then insert the basket in the unit. 3. Select DOUBLE STACK PRO. Select Zone 1. Turn the dial to select AIR FRY, set the temperature to 200°C, and set the time to 10 minutes. Press START/PAUSE to begin cooking. 4. Open the air fryer and flip the drumsticks. Cook for an additional 8 minutes. 5. Remove the cooked drumsticks from the air fryer. 6. In a small bowl, combine the honey and barbecue sauce. Drizzle the sauce over the drumsticks and serve.

Crunchy Chicken and Ranch Tortillas

Prep: 15 minutes   **Cook: 10 minutes**   **Serves: 4**

Ingredients:

2 (115g) boneless, skinless breasts
½ packet (30g) Hidden Valley Ranch seasoning mix
Chicken seasoning or rub
125g all-purpose flour
1 egg
55g breadcrumbs
Cooking oil
4 medium (8-inch) flour tortillas
55g shredded lettuce
3 tablespoons ranch dressing

Preparation:

1. With your knife blade parallel to the cutting board, slice the chicken breasts in half horizontally to create 4 thin cutlets. 2. Season the chicken cutlets with the ranch seasoning and chicken seasoning to taste. 3. In a bowl large enough to dip a chicken cutlet, beat the egg. In another bowl, place the flour. Put the breadcrumbs in a third bowl. 4. Insert a crisper plate in the Zone 1 basket and spray with cooking oil. 5. Dip each chicken cutlet in the flour, then the egg, and finally the breadcrumbs. 6. Place two chicken cutlets in the basket, spray the chicken with cooking oil. Then place one Stacked Meal Rack in the basket over the chicken cutlets. Place the remaining chicken cutlets on the rack and spray with cooking oil, then insert the basket in the unit. 7. Select DOUBLE STACK PRO. Select Zone 1. Turn the dial to select AIR FRY, set the temperature to 185°C, and set the time to 7 minutes. Press START/PAUSE to begin cooking. 8. Open the air fryer and flip the chicken. Cook for 3 to 4 minutes longer, until crisp. 9. Remove the cooked chicken from the air fryer and allow to cool for 2 to 3 minutes. 10. Cut the chicken into strips. Divide the chicken strips, shredded lettuce, and ranch dressing evenly among the tortillas and serve.

Garlicky Chicken Wings

⏱ **Prep: 10 minutes**   🍲 **Cook: 15 minutes**   ❖ **Serves: 4**

Ingredients:
8 whole chicken wings
1 teaspoon garlic powder
Chicken seasoning or rub
Pepper
Cooking oil

Preparation:
1. Season the wings with the garlic powder, chicken seasoning, and pepper to taste. 2. Insert a crisper plate in a basket, place the chicken wings in the basket and spray the chicken with cooking oil. Then insert the basket in Zone 1. The unit will default to Zone 1. Turn the dial to select AIR FRY, set the temperature to 200°C, and set the time to 10 minutes. Press START/PAUSE to begin cooking. 3. Remove the basket and shake it to ensure all of the chicken pieces will cook fully. 4. Return the basket and cook the chicken for an additional 5 minutes. 5. Cool before serving.

Spinach and Cream Cheese Stuffed Chicken

⏱ **Prep: 20 minutes**   🍲 **Cook: 10 minutes**   ❖ **Serves: 4**

Ingredients:
For the Filling:
75g cream cheese
30g chopped fresh spinach
For the Chicken:
4 (115g) boneless, skinless chicken breasts
Chicken seasoning or rub
Salt
Pepper
Cooking oil
1 teaspoon paprika

Preparation:
To make the filling: 1. In a small, microwave-safe bowl, heat the cream cheese in the microwave for 15 seconds to soften. 2. In a medium bowl, combine the cream cheese and the chopped spinach. Stir well. Set aside.
To make the chicken: 1. Cut 4 or 5 slits into each chicken breast without cutting all the way through. 2. Season the chicken with chicken seasoning, salt, and pepper to taste. 3. Insert a crisper plate in the Zone 1 basket and spray with cooking oil. Place 2 chicken breasts in the basket, then place one Stacked Meal Rack in the basket over the chicken breasts. Place the remaining chicken breasts on the rack, then insert the basket in the unit. 4. Select DOUBLE STACK PRO. Select Zone 1. Turn the dial to select AIR FRY, set the temperature to 185°C, and set the time to 7 minutes. Press START/PAUSE to begin cooking. 5. Open the air fryer and stuff the spinach and cream cheese mixture into the slits of the chicken. Sprinkle ½ teaspoon of paprika all over the stuffed chicken breasts. Cook for an additional 3 minutes. 6. Remove the cooked chicken from the air fryer and allow them to cool before serving.

| Chapter 4 Poultry

Chapter 5 Fish and Seafood

Crispy Fish Sticks 40

Steamboat Shrimp and Tomato Salad 40

Salty and Sweet Salmon 41

Coriander-Lime Shrimp 41

Savoury Salmon Croquettes 42

Beer-Battered Cod and Chips 42

Spicy Cajun Shrimp 43

Delicious Firecracker Shrimp 43

Crispy Fish Sticks

⏱ **Prep: 10 minutes**   🍲 **Cook: 8 minutes**   📚 **Serves: 4**

Ingredients:
225g fish fillets (pollock or cod)
salt (optional)
55g plain breadcrumbs
oil for misting or cooking spray

Preparation:
1. Cut fish fillets into "fingers" about ½ x 3 inches. Sprinkle with salt to taste, if desired. 2. Roll fish in breadcrumbs. Spray all sides with oil or cooking spray. 3. Insert a crisper plate in a basket, place fish in the basket, then insert the basket in Zone 1. The unit will default to Zone 1. Turn the dial to select AIR FRY, set the temperature to 200°C, and set the time to 8 minutes. Press START/PAUSE to begin cooking. Cook until golden brown and crispy.

Steamboat Shrimp and Tomato Salad

⏱ **Prep: 25 minutes**   🍲 **Cook: 4 minutes**   📚 **Serves: 4**

Ingredients:
24 small, raw shrimp, peeled and deveined
1 teaspoon lemon juice
¼ teaspoon Old Bay Seasoning
Steamboat Dressing:
110g mayonnaise
120g plain yoghurt
2 teaspoons freshly squeezed lemon juice (no substitutes)
2 teaspoons grated lemon rind
1 teaspoon dill weed, slightly crushed
½ teaspoon hot sauce
Salad:
300g romaine or Bibb lettuce, chopped or torn
30g red onion, cut into thin slivers
12 black olives, sliced
12 cherry or grape tomatoes, halved
1 medium avocado, sliced or cut into large chunks

Preparation:
1. Combine all dressing ingredients and mix well. Refrigerate while preparing shrimp and salad. 2. Sprinkle raw shrimp with lemon juice and Old Bay Seasoning. Use more Old Bay if you like your shrimp bold and spicy. 3. Insert a crisper plate in a basket, place the shrimp in the basket in a single layer, then insert the basket in Zone 1. The unit will default to Zone 1. Turn the dial to select AIR FRY, set the temperature to 200°C, and set the time to 4 minutes. Press START/PAUSE to begin cooking. 4. Remove shrimp from basket and place in refrigerator to cool. 5. Combine all salad ingredients and mix gently. Divide among 4 salad plates or bowls. 6. Top each salad with 6 shrimp and serve with dressing.

Salty and Sweet Salmon

⏱ Prep: 35 minutes   🍱 Cook: 10 minutes   ≡ Serves: 4

Ingredients:

4 salmon fillets (½-inch thick, 85g to 115g each)
cooking spray
Marinade:
3 tablespoons low-sodium soy sauce
3 tablespoons rice vinegar
3 tablespoons ketchup
3 tablespoons olive oil
3 tablespoons brown sugar
1 teaspoon garlic powder
½ teaspoon ground ginger

Preparation:

1. Mix all marinade ingredients until well blended. 2. Place the salmon in a sealable plastic bag or shallow container with lid. Pour marinade over the fish and turn to coat well. Refrigerate for 30 minutes. 3. Drain the marinade, and spray air fryer basket with cooking spray. 4. Insert a crisper plate in the Zone 1 basket and spray with cooking spray. Place 2 fillets in the basket, skin-side down. Then place one Stacked Meal Rack in the basket over the fillets. Place the remaining fillets on the rack, then insert the basket in the unit. 5. Select DOUBLE STACK PRO. Select Zone 1. Turn the dial to select ROAST, set the temperature to 180°C, and set the time to 10 minutes. Press START/PAUSE to begin cooking. Watch closely to avoid overcooking. Salmon is done when just beginning to flake and still very moist.

Coriander-Lime Shrimp

⏱ Prep: 10 minutes   🍱 Cook: 8 minutes   ≡ Serves: 4

Ingredients:

455g raw shrimp, peeled and deveined with tails on or off
10g chopped fresh coriander
Juice of 1 lime
1 egg
60g all-purpose flour
80g breadcrumbs
Salt
Pepper
Cooking oil
120ml cocktail sauce (optional)

Preparation:

1. Place the shrimp in a plastic bag and add the coriander and lime juice. Seal the bag. Shake to combine. Marinate in the refrigerator for 30 minutes. 2. In a small bowl, beat the egg. In another small bowl, place the flour. Place the breadcrumbs in a third small bowl, and season with salt and pepper to taste. 3. Spray the air fryer basket with cooking oil. 4. Remove the shrimp from the plastic bag. Dip each in the flour, then the egg, and then the breadcrumbs. 5. Insert a crisper plate in a basket and spray with cooking oil, place the shrimp in the basket. It is okay to stack them. Spray the shrimp with cooking oil. Then insert the basket in Zone 1. The unit will default to Zone 1. Turn the dial to select AIR FRY, set the temperature to 200°C, and set the time to 4 minutes. Press START/PAUSE to begin cooking. 6. Open the air fryer and flip the shrimp. Cook for an additional 4 minutes, or until crisp. 7. Cool before serving. Serve with cocktail sauce if desired.

Chapter 5 Fish and Seafood

Savoury Salmon Croquettes

⏱ **Prep: 5 minutes**   🍲 **Cook: 10 minutes**   ≋ **Serves: 6**

Ingredients:

1 can (420g) Alaskan pink salmon, drained and bones removed
1 egg, beaten
55g breadcrumbs
2 scallions, diced
1 teaspoon garlic powder
Salt
Pepper
Cooking oil

Preparation:

1. In a large bowl, combine the salmon, beaten egg, breadcrumbs, and scallions. Season with the garlic powder and salt and pepper to taste. 2. Form the mixture into 6 patties. 3. Insert a crisper plate in a basket. Place the croquettes in the basket. It is okay to stack them. Spray the croquettes with cooking oil. Then insert the basket in Zone 1. The unit will default to Zone 1. Turn the dial to select AIR FRY, set the temperature to 200°C, and set the time to 7 minutes. Press START/PAUSE to begin cooking. 4. Open the air fryer and flip the patties. Cook for an additional 3 to 4 minutes, or until golden brown. 5. Serve.

Beer-Battered Cod and Chips

⏱ **Prep: 10 minutes**   🍲 **Cook: 15 minutes**   ≋ **Serves: 4**

Ingredients:

2 eggs
235ml malty beer, such as Pabst Blue Ribbon
125g all-purpose flour
65g cornstarch
1 teaspoon garlic powder
Salt
Pepper
Cooking oil
4 (115g) cod fillets

Preparation:

1. In a medium bowl, beat the eggs with the beer. In another medium bowl, combine the flour and cornstarch, and season with the garlic powder and salt and pepper to taste. 2. Dip each cod fillet in the flour and cornstarch mixture and then in the egg and beer mixture. Dip the cod in the flour and cornstarch a second time. 3. Insert a crisper plate in the Zone 1 basket and spray with cooking oil. Place 2 cod fillets in the basket, do not stack. Then place one Stacked Meal Rack in the basket over the cod fillets. Place the remaining cod fillets on the rack, then insert the basket in the unit. 4. Select DOUBLE STACK PRO. Select Zone 1. Turn the dial to select AIR FRY, set the temperature to 200°C, and set the time to 15 minutes. Press START/PAUSE to begin cooking. Flip halfway through the cooking time. 5. Remove the cooked cod from the air fryer, then repeat steps 4 and 5 for the remaining fillets. 6. Serve with French fries or prepare air-fried frozen fries. Frozen fries will need to be cooked for 18 to 20 minutes at 400°F. 7. Cool before serving.

| Chapter 5 Fish and Seafood

Spicy Cajun Shrimp

⏰ **Prep: 5 minutes**   🍲 **Cook: 6 minutes**   ❖ **Serves: 2**

Ingredients:

340g uncooked medium shrimp, peeled and deveined
1 teaspoon cayenne pepper
1 teaspoon Old Bay seasoning
½ teaspoon smoked paprika
2 tablespoons olive oil
1 teaspoon salt

Preparation:

1. In a medium mixing bowl, combine the shrimp, cayenne pepper, Old Bay, paprika, olive oil, and salt. Toss the shrimp in the oil and spices until the shrimp is thoroughly coated with both. 2. Insert a crisper plate in a basket, place the shrimp in the basket, then insert the basket in Zone 1. The unit will default to Zone 1. Turn the dial to select AIR FRY, set the temperature to 200°C, and set the time to 3 minutes. Press START/PAUSE to begin cooking. 3. Shake the shrimp and cook for another 3 minutes. 4. Check that the shrimp are done. When they are cooked through, the flesh will be opaque. Add additional time if needed. 5. Plate, serve, and enjoy!

Delicious Firecracker Shrimp

⏰ **Prep: 10 minutes**   🍲 **Cook: 8 minutes**   ❖ **Serves: 4**

Ingredients:

For the Shrimp:
455g raw shrimp, peeled and deveined
Salt
Pepper
1 egg
60g all-purpose flour
75g panko breadcrumbs
Cooking oil
For the Firecracker Sauce:
80g sour cream
2 tablespoons Sriracha
60ml sweet chilli sauce

Preparation:

To make the shrimp: 1. Season the shrimp with salt and pepper to taste. 2. In a small bowl, beat the egg. 3. In another small bowl, place the flour. In a third small bowl, add the panko breadcrumbs. 4. Dip the shrimp in the flour, then the egg, and then the breadcrumbs. 5. Insert a crisper plate in a basket and spray with cooking oil. Place the shrimp in the air fryer basket. It is okay to stack them. Spray the shrimp with cooking oil. Then insert the basket in Zone 1. The unit will default to Zone 1. Turn the dial to select AIR FRY, set the temperature to 200°C, and set the time to 4 minutes. Press START/PAUSE to begin cooking. 6. Open the air fryer and flip the shrimp. Cook for an additional 4 minutes or until crisp.
To make the firecracker sauce: 1. While the shrimp is cooking, make the firecracker sauce: In a small bowl, combine the sour cream, Sriracha, and sweet chilli sauce. Mix well. 2. Serve with the shrimp.

Chapter 6 Beef, Pork, and Lamb

Cumin Pork Tenderloin and Potatoes	45
Lamb Kofta with Tzatziki	45
Flavourful Kofta Kebabs	46
Chinese-Style Baby Back Ribs	46
Italian Cheese Sausage Meatballs	47
Authentic Carne Asada	47
Beef Sliders	48
The Best Steak Frites	48
Spicy Pork Bulgogi	49
Mint Lamb Kebabs	49
Hoisin Barbecue Country-Style Pork Ribs	50
Savoury Meatballs with Marinara	50
Cheese Meatballs and Potatoes	51
Bulgogi Burgers with Gochujang Mayonnaise	52
Beef-Rice Stuffed Peppers	53
Teriyaki Baby Back Ribs	54
Sonoran Style Hot Dogs	55
Classic Natchitoches Meat Pie	56

Cumin Pork Tenderloin and Potatoes

⏱ Prep: 15 minutes   🍲 Cook: 20 minutes   ⚇ Serves: 6

Ingredients:

3 tablespoons ground cumin
1 teaspoon chilli powder
1 teaspoon kosher salt
¼ teaspoon black pepper
2 cloves garlic, minced
455g pork tenderloin, cut into 2 pieces
Vegetable oil for spraying
455g Yukon gold potatoes, quartered
1 tablespoon extra-virgin olive oil

Preparation:

1. Combine the spices and garlic in a small bowl. Transfer 1 tablespoon of the spice mixture to another bowl and set it aside to season the potatoes. Rub both pieces of the tenderloin with the remaining seasoning mixture. Set aside. 2. Put the potatoes in a medium bowl. Add the reserved tablespoon of seasoning mixture and the olive oil. Toss gently to ensure the potatoes are evenly coated. 3. Insert the crisper plates in the baskets and spray with oil. Place both pieces of tenderloin in the Zone 1 basket and spray lightly with oil. 4. Place the potatoes in the Zone 2 basket, then insert the baskets in the unit. 5. Select Zone 1, then use the dial to select ROAST, set the temperature to 180°C, and set the time to 20 minutes. 6. Select Zone 2, then use the dial to select AIR FRY, set the temperature to 200°C, and set the time to 10 minutes. Select SMART FINISH, then press START/PAUSE to begin cooking (Zone 2 will read HOLD until it's time to start cooking). 7. Flip the pork tenderloin halfway through. Toss the potatoes once halfway through cooking, until golden brown. 8. Serve immediately alongside the pork tenderloin.

Lamb Kofta with Tzatziki

⏱ Prep: 15 minutes   🍲 Cook: 10 minutes   ⚇ Serves: 4

Ingredients:

455g ground lamb
½ onion, grated
15g chopped fresh flat-leaf parsley, mint, or a combination
1 teaspoon kosher salt
½ teaspoon cumin
½ teaspoon coriander
½ teaspoon paprika
¼ teaspoon allspice
¼ teaspoon cinnamon
Vegetable oil for spraying
Tzatziki for serving

Preparation:

1. Combine the lamb, onion, herbs, salt, and spices in a medium bowl and mix thoroughly. Form the lamb mixture into 8 equal, tightly packed patties. Place the patties on a plate, cover, and refrigerate for at least 30 minutes and up to 8 hours. 2. Insert a crisper plate in the Zone 1 basket and spray with oil, place the patties in a single layer in the basket, then place one Stacked Meal Rack in the basket over the patties. Place the remaining patties on the rack, then insert the basket in the unit. 3. Select DOUBLE STACK PRO. Select Zone 1. Turn the dial to select AIR FRY, set the temperature to 200°C, and set the time to 10 minutes. Press START/PAUSE to begin cooking, flipping the patties once halfway through cooking. Cook until the internal temperature reaches 63°C. 4. Remove the patties to a paper towel–lined plate to absorb excess oil. Serve the patties warm with Tzatziki.

Chapter 6 Beef, Pork, and Lamb | 45

Flavourful Kofta Kebabs

⏱ **Prep: 15 minutes**　🍲 **Cook: 10 minutes**　📚 **Serves: 4**

Ingredients:

455g 85% lean ground beef
15g chopped fresh parsley, plus more for garnish
2 tablespoons Kofta Kebab Spice Mix
1 tablespoon vegetable oil
1 tablespoon minced garlic
1 teaspoon kosher salt

Preparation:

1. In the bowl of a stand mixer fitted with the paddle attachment, combine the ground beef, parsley, spice mix, vegetable oil, garlic, and salt. Mix on low speed until you have a sticky mess of spiced meat. If you have time, let the mixture stand at room temperature for 30 minutes (or cover and refrigerate for up to a day or two, until you're ready to make the kebabs). 2. Divide the meat into four equal portions. Form each into a long sausage shape. 3. Insert a crisper plate in a basket, place the kebabs in a single layer in the basket, then insert the basket in Zone 1. The unit will default to Zone 1. Turn the dial to select AIR FRY, set the temperature to 175°C, and set the time to 10 minutes. Press START/PAUSE to begin cooking. Use a meat thermometer to ensure the kebabs have reached an internal temperature of 70°C (medium). 4. Transfer the kebabs to a serving platter. Sprinkle with additional parsley and serve.

Chinese-Style Baby Back Ribs

⏱ **Prep: 30 minutes**　🍲 **Cook: 30 minutes**　📚 **Serves: 4**

Ingredients:

1 tablespoon toasted sesame oil
1 tablespoon fermented black bean paste
1 tablespoon Shaoxing wine (rice cooking wine)
1 tablespoon dark soy sauce
1 tablespoon agave nectar or honey
1 teaspoon minced garlic
1 teaspoon minced fresh ginger
1 (680g) slab baby back ribs, cut into individual ribs

Preparation:

1. In a large bowl, stir together the sesame oil, black bean paste, wine, soy sauce, agave, garlic, and ginger. Add the ribs and toss well to coat. Marinate at room temperature for 30 minutes, or cover and refrigerate for up to 24 hours. 2. Insert a crisper plate in a basket, place the ribs in the basket; discard the marinade. Then insert the basket in Zone 1. The unit will default to Zone 1. Turn the dial to select AIR FRY, set the temperature to 175°C, and set the time to 30 minutes. Press START/PAUSE to begin cooking. 3. Serve warm.

| Chapter 6 Beef, Pork, and Lamb

Italian Cheese Sausage Meatballs

⏰ **Prep: 10 minutes**　🍲 **Cook: 20 minutes**　🔷 **Serves: 4**

Ingredients:

225g bulk Italian sausage
225g 85% lean ground beef
50g shredded sharp cheddar cheese
½ teaspoon onion powder
½ teaspoon garlic powder
½ teaspoon black pepper

Preparation:

1. In a large bowl, gently mix the sausage, ground beef, cheese, onion powder, garlic powder, and pepper until well combined. 2. Form the mixture into 16 meatballs. Insert a crisper plate in the Zone 1 basket, place half of the meatballs in a single layer in the basket, then place one Stacked Meal Rack in the basket over the meatballs. Place the remaining meatballs on the rack, then insert the basket in the unit. 3. Select DOUBLE STACK PRO. Select Zone 1. Turn the dial to select AIR FRY, set the temperature to 175°C, and set the time to 20 minutes. Press START/PAUSE to begin cooking, turning the meatballs halfway through the cooking time. Use a meat thermometer to ensure the meatballs have reached an internal temperature of 70°C (medium).

Authentic Carne Asada

⏰ **Prep: 10 minutes**　🍲 **Cook: 8 minutes**　🔷 **Serves: 4**

Ingredients:

Juice of 2 limes
1 orange, peeled and seeded
25g fresh coriander leaves
1 jalapeño, diced
2 tablespoons vegetable oil
2 tablespoons apple cider vinegar
2 teaspoons ancho chilli powder
2 teaspoons sugar
1 teaspoon kosher salt
1 teaspoon cumin seeds
1 teaspoon coriander seeds
680g skirt steak, cut into 3 pieces

Preparation:

1. In a blender, combine the lime juice, orange, coriander, jalapeño, vegetable oil, vinegar, chilli powder, sugar, salt, cumin, and coriander. Blend until smooth. 2. Place the steak in a resealable plastic bag. Pour the marinade over the steak and seal the bag. Let stand at room temperature for 30 minutes or cover and refrigerate for up to 24 hours. 3. Insert a crisper plate in the Zone 1 basket, place 2 pieces of steaks in the basket, then place one Stacked Meal Rack in the basket over the steaks. Place the remaining 1 piece of steak on the rack, discard the marinade. Then insert the basket in the unit. 4. Select DOUBLE STACK PRO. Select Zone 1. Turn the dial to select AIR FRY, set the temperature to 200°C, and set the time to 8 minutes. Press START/PAUSE to begin cooking. 5. Use a meat thermometer to ensure the steak has reached an internal temperature of 60°C. (It is critical to not overcook the skirt steak to avoid toughening the meat.) 6. Transfer the steak to a cutting board and let it rest for 10 minutes. Slice across the grain and serve.

Beef Sliders

⏱ **Prep: 10 minutes**   🍲 **Cook: 8 minutes**   ⊗ **Serves: 4**

Ingredients:
455g lean ground sirloin beef (90% lean recommended)
½ teaspoon kosher salt
Pinch of freshly ground black pepper
6 whole wheat dinner rolls, sliced

Preparation:
1. Form the ground beef into 6 patties and season with salt and black pepper. 2. Insert a crisper plate in the Zone 1 basket and spray with nonstick cooking spray. Place 3 patties in one layer in the basket, then place one Stacked Meal Rack in the basket over the patties. Place the remaining patties on the rack, then insert the basket in the unit. 3. Select DOUBLE STACK PRO. Select Zone 1. Turn the dial to select AIR FRY, set the temperature to 180°C, and set the time to 8 minutes. Press START/PAUSE to begin cooking. 4. Remove the burgers from the fryer, place on a plate lined with a paper towel, and allow to cool for 5–10 minutes. Place the burgers on the whole wheat dinner rolls and top as desired before serving.

The Best Steak Frites

⏱ **Prep: 15 minutes**   🍲 **Cook: 15 minutes**   ⊗ **Serves: 4**

Ingredients:
225g russet or Yukon gold potatoes
1½ teaspoons vegetable oil
½ teaspoon salt
⅝ teaspoon pepper
2 tablespoons mayonnaise
¼ small shallot, finely chopped
1 teaspoon lemon juice
½ teaspoon finely chopped fresh tarragon, plus more for garnish
2 thin (⅜-inch-thick) boneless top sirloin steaks (about 340g)

Preparation:
1. Cut potatoes into ¼-inch sticks; soak in water for 10 minutes. Drain and pat dry. Toss potatoes, oil, and ¼ teaspoon each salt and pepper. 2. Combine mayonnaise, shallot, 1 teaspoon water, lemon juice, tarragon, and ⅛ teaspoon pepper. Season steaks with ¼ teaspoon each salt and pepper. 3. Insert the crisper plates in the baskets. Place the potato sticks in the Zone 1 basket. Place the steaks in the Zone 2 basket, then insert the baskets in the unit. 4. Select Zone 1, then use the dial to select AIR FRY, set the temperature to 190°C, and set the time to 15 minutes. 5. Select Zone 2, then use the dial to select ROAST, set the temperature to 200°C, and set the time to 6 minutes. Select SMART FINISH, then press START/PAUSE to begin cooking (Zone 2 will read HOLD until it's time to start cooking). 6. Shake the Zone 1 basket twice and turn the steaks once during cooking. 7. Place the steaks on a board to rest for 2 minutes. Serve fries with steak and mayo. Garnish with chopped tarragon.

▶ | Chapter 6 Beef, Pork, and Lamb

Spicy Pork Bulgogi

⏱ Prep: 30 minutes   🍳 Cook: 15 minutes   ❖ Serves: 4

Ingredients:

1 onion, thinly sliced
2 tablespoons gochujang (Korean red chilli paste)
1 tablespoon minced fresh ginger
1 tablespoon minced garlic
1 tablespoon soy sauce
1 tablespoon Shaoxing wine (rice cooking wine)
1 tablespoon toasted sesame oil
1 teaspoon sugar
¼ to 1 teaspoon cayenne pepper or gochugaru (Korean ground red pepper)
455g boneless pork shoulder, cut into ½-inch-thick slices
1 tablespoon sesame seeds
25g sliced scallions

Preparation:

1. In a large bowl, combine the onion, gochujang, ginger, garlic, soy sauce, wine, sesame oil, sugar, and cayenne. Add the pork and toss to coat. Marinate at room temperature for 30 minutes, or cover and refrigerate for up to 24 hours. 2. Insert a crisper plate in a basket. Arrange the pork and onion slices in the air-fryer basket; discard the marinade. Then insert the basket in Zone 1. The unit will default to Zone 1. Turn the dial to select AIR FRY, set the temperature to 200°C, and set the time to 15 minutes. Press START/PAUSE to begin cooking, turning the pork halfway through the cooking time. 3. Arrange the pork on a serving platter. Sprinkle with the sesame seeds and scallions and serve.

Mint Lamb Kebabs

⏱ Prep: 20 minutes   🍳 Cook: 14 minutes   ❖ Serves: 4

Ingredients:

455g ground lamb
80g finely minced onion
15g chopped fresh mint
5g chopped fresh coriander
1 tablespoon minced garlic
½ teaspoon ground turmeric
½ teaspoon cayenne pepper
¼ teaspoon ground cardamom
¼ teaspoon ground cinnamon
1 teaspoon kosher salt

Preparation:

1. In the bowl of a stand mixer fitted with the paddle attachment, combine the lamb, onion, mint, coriander, garlic, turmeric, cayenne, cardamom, cinnamon, and salt. Mix on low speed until you have a sticky mess of spiced meat. If you have time, let the mixture stand at room temperature for 30 minutes (or cover and refrigerate for up to a day or two, until you're ready to make the kebabs). 2. Divide the meat into eight equal portions. Form each into a long sausage shape. 3. Insert a crisper plate in the Zone 1 basket, place half of the kebabs in a single layer in the basket, then place one Stacked Meal Rack in the basket over the kebabs. Place the remaining kebabs on the rack, then insert the basket in the unit. 4. Select DOUBLE STACK PRO. Select Zone 1. Turn the dial to select AIR FRY, set the temperature to 175°C, and set the time to 10 minutes. Press START/PAUSE to begin cooking. 5. Increase the air-fryer temperature to 200°C and cook for 3 to 4 minutes more to brown the kebabs. Use a meat thermometer to ensure the kebabs have reached an internal temperature of 70°C (medium).

Hoisin Barbecue Country-Style Pork Ribs

⏲ Prep: 15 minutes   🍲 Cook: 30 minutes   ≋ Serves: 4

Ingredients:

80ml soy sauce
80ml apple cider vinegar
2 tablespoons brown sugar
1 teaspoon ground ginger
½ teaspoon garlic powder
4 bone-in country-style pork ribs (about 910g)
3 tablespoons barbecue sauce
2 tablespoons Hoisin sauce
Slaw, for serving
Sesame seeds, for garnish (optional)

Preparation:

1. Combine soy sauce, vinegar, sugar, ginger, garlic powder, and 60ml water in a heavy food storage bag. Add ribs, shake to combine, push out all air, and seal. Marinate in the refrigerator for 2 to 8 hours; turn over the bag occasionally. Drain well and discard the marinade. In a small bowl, mix together barbecue sauce and Hoisin. 2. Insert the crisper plates in the baskets. Divide the pork ribs evenly between both baskets, then insert the baskets in the unit. The unit will default to Zone 1. Turn the dial to select AIR FRY. Set the temperature to 175°C and set the time to 30 minutes. Press the MATCH COOK button to copy Zone 1's settings to Zone 2. Press START/ PAUSE to begin cooking in both zones, turning over ribs using tongs every 10 minutes and brushing lightly with the Hoisin-BBQ sauce. Brush with the remaining sauce. 3. Serve with slaw. Garnish with sesame seeds, if desired.

Savoury Meatballs with Marinara

⏲ Prep: 10 minutes   🍲 Cook: 8 minutes   ≋ Serves: 4

Ingredients:

455g lean ground sirloin beef (90% lean recommended)
2 tablespoons seasoned breadcrumbs
1 large egg, beaten
¼ teaspoon kosher salt
265g marinara sauce (for serving)

Preparation:

1. In a medium bowl, combine the ground beef, seasoned breadcrumbs, egg, and kosher salt, then form the mixture into sixteen 30g balls. 2. Insert a crisper plate in the Zone 1 basket and spray with nonstick cooking spray. Place half of the meatballs in the basket, then place one Stacked Meal Rack in the basket over the meatballs. Place the remaining meatballs on the rack, then insert the basket in the unit. 3. Select DOUBLE STACK PRO. Select Zone 1. Turn the dial to select AIR FRY, set the temperature to 180°C, and set the time to 8 minutes. Press START/PAUSE to begin cooking. Cook until the internal temperature reaches 70°C. 4. Remove the meatballs from the fryer, place on a plate lined with a paper towel, and allow to cool for 5 minutes. Serve with the marinara sauce.

Chapter 6 Beef, Pork, and Lamb

Cheese Meatballs and Potatoes

⏰ **Prep: 20 minutes**   🍲 **Cook: 14 minutes**   ≋ **Serves: 4**

Ingredients:

455g red potatoes, cut into 1-inch chunks
2 teaspoons olive oil
½ teaspoon salt
⅜ teaspoon pepper
455g lean ground beef (90%)
185g crumbled feta cheese
½ small red onion, grated
35g Italian seasoned breadcrumbs
15g chopped fresh parsley leaves
1 large egg, lightly beaten
2 teaspoons dried oregano
120g prepared tzatziki sauce
Lemon slices and parsley, for serving

Preparation:

1. In a medium-size bowl, toss potatoes with oil, ¼ teaspoon salt, and ⅛ teaspoon pepper. 2. In a large bowl, mix ground beef, feta, red onion, breadcrumbs, parsley, egg, oregano and ¼ teaspoon each salt and pepper. Form into 12 balls and thread onto skewers. 3. Insert the crisper plates in the baskets. Place the potatoes in the Zone 1 basket. Place meatballs in the Zone 2 basket, then insert the baskets in the unit. 4. Select Zone 1, then use the dial to select AIR FRY, set the temperature to 200°C, and set the time to 14 minutes. 5. Select Zone 2, then use the dial to select AIR FRY, set the temperature to 190°C, and set the time to 10 minutes. Select SMART FINISH, then press START/PAUSE to begin cooking (Zone 2 will read HOLD until it's time to start cooking). 6. Toss the potatoes a few times. Remove potatoes and meatballs to a plate. 7. Serve with tzatziki and lemon slices. Garnish with additional parsley.

Chapter 6 Beef, Pork, and Lamb

Bulgogi Burgers with Gochujang Mayonnaise

Prep: 15 minutes Cook: 10 minutes Serves: 4

Ingredients:

For the Burgers:
455g 85% lean ground beef
25g chopped scallions
2 tablespoons gochujang (Korean red chilli paste)
1 tablespoon dark soy sauce
2 teaspoons minced garlic
2 teaspoons minced fresh ginger
2 teaspoons sugar
1 tablespoon toasted sesame oil
½ teaspoon kosher salt

For the Gochujang Mayonnaise:
55g mayonnaise
25g chopped scallions
1 tablespoon gochujang (Korean red chilli paste)
1 tablespoon toasted sesame oil
2 teaspoons sesame seeds
4 hamburger buns

Preparation:

1. For the burgers: In a large bowl, mix the ground beef, scallions, gochujang, soy sauce, garlic, ginger, sugar, sesame oil, and salt. Marinate at room temperature for 30 minutes, or cover and refrigerate for up to 24 hours. 2. Divide the meat into four portions and form them into round patties. Make a slight depression in the middle of each patty with your thumb to prevent them from puffing up into a dome shape while cooking. 3. Insert a crisper plate in a basket. Place the patties in a single layer in the basket, then insert the basket in Zone 1. The unit will default to Zone 1. Turn the dial to select AIR FRY, set the temperature to 175°C, and set the time to 10 minutes. Press START/PAUSE to begin cooking. 4. Meanwhile, for the gochujang mayonnaise: Stir together the mayonnaise, scallions, gochujang, sesame oil, and sesame seeds. 5. At the end of the cooking time, use a meat thermometer to ensure the burgers have reached an internal temperature of 70°C (medium). 6. To serve, place the burgers on the buns and top with the mayonnaise.

Beef-Rice Stuffed Peppers

⏱ **Prep: 15 minutes**   🍲 **Cook: 30 minutes**   ❖ **Serves: 4**

Ingredients:

2 tablespoons extra-virgin olive oil
1 yellow onion, diced
3 cloves garlic, minced
340 g ground beef
2 teaspoons kosher salt
Pinch red pepper flakes
2 medium tomatoes or 1 large tomato
35g pine nuts
35g raisins
3 tablespoons red wine vinegar
165g cooked rice
4 bell peppers
Vegetable oil for spraying
150g grated mozzarella cheese

Preparation:

1. Heat the olive oil in a large, deep skillet over medium heat. When the oil is shimmering, add the onion and sauté until softened, about 5 minutes. Add the garlic and sauté for an additional minute. Add the ground beef, salt, and red pepper flakes and cook until the meat is no longer pink, about 6 minutes. If the meat has given off a lot of grease, carefully remove it from the skillet with a spoon. 2. Slice off the stem end of the tomatoes and grate them using the coarse side of a box grater. Discard the skin. Add the tomato pulp, pine nuts, raisins, and vinegar to the meat mixture and sauté a few additional minutes to thicken. Add the cooked rice and stir to combine. Remove from the heat and set aside. 3. Insert a crisper plate in a basket. Cut off the top third of the peppers and remove the seeds and inner membranes. Divide the meat mixture evenly among the 4 peppers. Place the tops back on the peppers and place them carefully in the basket of the air fryer. Spray or brush the outsides and tops of the peppers with oil. 4. Then insert the basket in Zone 1. The unit will default to Zone 1. Turn the dial to select AIR FRY, set the temperature to 190°C, and set the time to 15 minutes. Press START/PAUSE to begin cooking, rotating the peppers halfway through. Remove the tops and add 40g grated mozzarella to each pepper. Cook until the cheese is melted and browned, about 4 minutes. 5. Serve immediately.

Teriyaki Baby Back Ribs

⏰ **Prep: 15 minutes**   🍲 **Cook: 1 hour**   📚 **Serves: 4**

Ingredients:

1 teaspoon Chinese five-spice powder
½ teaspoon garlic powder
1 teaspoon kosher salt
1 teaspoon black pepper
1135g to 1360g rack baby back ribs, cut into 4 pieces
60ml soy sauce, preferably low-sodium
1 tablespoon brown sugar
1 tablespoon vegetable oil
½ tablespoon grated fresh ginger
1 clove garlic, minced
3 teaspoons rice vinegar
1 teaspoon toasted sesame oil

Preparation:

1. Combine the Chinese five-spice powder, garlic powder, salt, and pepper in a small bowl and whisk to combine. Place each rib section on a large piece of foil and sprinkle all over with the spice mixture. Wrap the foil tightly around each rib section. 2. Insert a crisper plate in a basket, arrange the foil-wrapped ribs in the basket, then insert the basket in Zone 1. The unit will default to Zone 1. Turn the dial to select ROAST, set the temperature to 120°C, and set the time to 50 minutes. Press START/PAUSE to begin cooking. 3. While the ribs are cooking, combine the soy sauce, brown sugar, oil, rice vinegar, ginger, garlic, and sesame oil in a small bowl and whisk until combined. 4. After 50 minutes, use tongs to remove the ribs from the air fryer and place on a rimmed baking sheet. Allow the ribs to cool slightly, then carefully remove from the foil. 5. Brush the ribs evenly with the sauce mixture and return to the air fryer. Set the temperature to 200°C and cook for 10 minutes, occasionally basting the ribs with additional sauce. The ribs should be crispy, tender, and slightly charred when cooked. Brush the cooked ribs with any remaining sauce and serve immediately.

Chapter 6 Beef, Pork, and Lamb

Sonoran Style Hot Dogs

Prep: 15 minutes   **Cook: 12 minutes**   **Serves: 4**

Ingredients:

4 large hot dogs
4 slices bacon (not thick-cut)
2 tablespoons unsalted butter, at room temperature
4 fresh bolillo rolls or good-quality hot dog buns
120g refried beans, warmed
1 avocado, diced
1 Roma tomato, diced
½ small red onion, diced
60ml Mexican crema, thinned with 1 tablespoon milk
Fresh coriander leaves, for garnish
Lime wedges, for garnish
Hot sauce, for serving

Preparation:

1. Wrap each hot dog with a slice of bacon and secure with toothpicks at each end. Place the hot dogs on a plate and refrigerate for 30 minutes to help the bacon adhere to the hot dogs. While the hot dogs chill, spread butter on the cut portion of each bun. 2. Insert a crisper plate in a basket, place the hot dogs in the basket, then insert the basket in Zone 1. The unit will default to Zone 1. Turn the dial to select AIR FRY, set the temperature to 180°C, and set the time to 8 minutes. Press START/PAUSE to begin cooking. 3. Open the air fryer and turn the hot dogs to ensure they are cooking evenly on all sides. Cook for an additional 2 minutes until the bacon is crisp and golden and the hot dog is plump. 4. Transfer the hot dogs to a plate and keep warm. Place the buttered buns in the air fryer and cook at 180°C for 1 to 2 minutes, until the buns are warm and the butter is melted. 5. To assemble, spread 2 tablespoons of refried beans into each bun. Add a bacon-wrapped hot dog. Top with diced avocado, tomato, onion, and a drizzle of Mexican crema. Garnish with coriander leaves; serve with lime wedges and hot sauce.

Classic Natchitoches Meat Pie

⏱ **Prep: 30 minutes** 🍲 **Cook: 40 minutes** ❖ **Serves: 4**

Ingredients:

Dough:
280g all-purpose flour
1¼ teaspoons kosher salt
4 tablespoons cold unsalted butter, cubed (or 8 tablespoons butter if you prefer not to use shortening)
4 tablespoons cold vegetable shortening, cubed
1 egg
120ml ice water
2 teaspoons red wine vinegar

Filling:
2 tablespoons vegetable or canola oil
½ red onion, diced
1 red bell pepper, diced
2 ribs celery, diced
Kosher salt and pepper
2 cloves garlic, minced
455g ground beef or 225g each ground beef and ground pork
1 tablespoon all-purpose flour
1 teaspoon paprika
1 teaspoon oregano
¼ teaspoon cayenne pepper
1 tablespoon tomato paste
235ml chicken or beef broth
½ teaspoon Worcestershire sauce
Dash Tabasco
1 egg beaten with 1 tablespoon water

Preparation:

1. To make the pie dough, mix together the flour and salt in a food processor and pulse a few times to combine. Add the butter and shortening and pulse until the mixture resembles coarse crumbs. Add the egg. Whisk together the ice water and vinegar and add 8 tablespoons to the flour. Pulse a few additional times. Take a small handful of the dough and pinch it to see if it holds together. If it does not, add more water until the dough holds together when squeezed. Turn the dough out onto a floured board and knead until it comes together in a ball. Wrap in plastic and refrigerate for at least 1 hour and up to several days. 2. To make the filling, heat the oil in a large, deep skillet over medium heat. Add the onion, red pepper, and celery and season with salt. Sauté until softened, about 5 minutes. Add the garlic and sauté for 1 additional minute. Add the ground beef (or ground beef and pork) and cook, using a wooden spoon to break up the meat, until the meat is no longer pink, 6 to 8 minutes. Season with salt and pepper. 3. Add the flour and spices and stir to combine. Sauté until fragrant, 2 to 3 minutes. Add the tomato paste, broth, Worcestershire sauce, and Tabasco and stir. Scrape up any browned bits that may have accumulated from the bottom of the pan. Simmer until most of the liquid has evaporated and the meat is covered in a thick gravy. Taste and adjust the seasoning. Remove from the heat and allow to cool completely before proceeding. 4. Divide the dough into 4 equal parts and roll each into a ball. Working with 1 piece at a time, roll the dough on a well-floured board to a circle of 7 to 8 inches (18 to 20 cm) in diameter and ⅛ to ¼ inch (3 to 6 mm) thick. Scoop half of the meat filling into the centre of the dough. Fold the dough over into a half-moon shape, line up the edges, and press them to seal. Crimp the edges shut by pinching them with the tines of a fork. Repeat with the remaining dough and filling. Place the filled pies on a parchment paper–lined baking sheet. (Pies may be filled ahead of time and chilled until ready to cook.) 5. Brush the tops of the pies with the egg wash and cut 2 small slits for venting in each pie. 6. Insert a crisper plate in the Zone 1 basket and spray with oil, place the two filled pies in the basket in one layer, then place one Stacked Meal Rack in the basket over the pies. Place the remaining 2 pies on the rack, then insert the basket in the unit. 7. Select DOUBLE STACK PRO. Select Zone 1. Turn the dial to select BAKE, set the temperature to 180°C, and set the time to 25 minutes. Press START/PAUSE to begin cooking. Bake until the crust is glossy and golden brown and the filling bubbles. If the pies are sticking, carefully remove them using a thin, nonstick-safe spatula. Serve immediately.

Chapter 7 Desserts

Almond-Baked Pears 58

Pecan-Stuffed Apple 58

Dark Brownies 59

Fluffy Chocolate Cake 59

Homemade Custard 60

Chocolate Chip Cookies 60

Crunch S'mores 61

Chocolate-Frosted Doughnuts 61

Apple Hand Pies 62

Pumpkin Fritters 63

Almond-Baked Pears

⏱ **Prep: 10 minutes**   🍲 **Cook: 15 minutes**   ≋ **Serves: 4**

▶ **Ingredients:**

Yoghurt Topping:
1 container vanilla Greek yoghurt (140g–170g)
¼ teaspoon almond flavouring
2 whole pears
20g crushed Biscoff cookies (approx. 4 cookies)
1 tablespoon sliced almonds
1 tablespoon butter

▶ **Preparation:**

1. Stir almond flavouring into yoghurt and set aside while preparing pears. 2. Halve each pear and spoon out the core. 3. Insert a crisper plate in a basket, place the pear halves in the basket. 4. Stir together the cookie crumbs and almonds. Place a quarter of this mixture into the hollow of each pear half. 5. Cut butter into 4 pieces and place one piece on top of the crumb mixture in each pear. 6. Then insert the basket in Zone 1. The unit will default to Zone 1. Turn the dial to select BAKE, set the temperature to 180°C, and set the time to 15 minutes. Press START/PAUSE to begin cooking. Bake until pears have cooked through but are still slightly firm. 7. Serve pears warm with a dollop of yoghurt topping.

Pecan-Stuffed Apple

⏱ **Prep: 10 minutes**   🍲 **Cook: 20 minutes**   ≋ **Serves: 6**

▶ **Ingredients:**

3 small Honey Crisp or other baking apples
3 tablespoons maple syrup
3 tablespoons chopped pecans
1 tablespoon firm butter, cut into 6 pieces

▶ **Preparation:**

1. Wash apples well and dry them. 2. Split apples in half. Remove the core and a little of the flesh to make a cavity for the pecans. 3. Insert a crisper plate in a basket, place apple halves in the basket, cut side up. 4. Spoon 1½ teaspoons of pecans into each cavity. 5. Spoon ½ tablespoon maple syrup over pecans in each apple. 6. Top each apple with ½ teaspoon butter. 7. Then insert the basket in Zone 1. The unit will default to Zone 1. Turn the dial to select BAKE, set the temperature to 180°C, and set the time to 20 minutes. Press START/PAUSE to begin cooking. Bake until the apples are tender.

Chapter 7 Desserts

Dark Brownies

⏱ Prep: 10 minutes 🍲 Cook: 12 minutes ◆ Serves: 4

Ingredients:

1 egg
95g granulated sugar
¼ teaspoon salt
½ teaspoon vanilla
55g butter, melted
30g flour, plus 2 tablespoons
20g cocoa
cooking spray
Optional
vanilla ice cream
caramel sauce
whipped cream

Preparation:

1. Beat together egg, sugar, salt, and vanilla until light. 2. Add melted butter and mix well. 3. Stir in flour and cocoa. 4. Spray a round baking pan that fits your air fryer lightly with cooking spray. 5. Spread batter in pan. Place the pan in the basket, then insert the basket in Zone 1. The unit will default to Zone 1. Turn the dial to select BAKE, set the temperature to 165°C, and set the time to 12 minutes. Press START/PAUSE to begin cooking. 6. Cool and cut into 4 large squares or 16 small brownie bites. Serve with vanilla ice cream, caramel sauce or whipped cream, if desired.

Fluffy Chocolate Cake

⏱ Prep: 10 minutes 🍲 Cook: 20 minutes ◆ Serves: 8

Ingredients:

95g sugar
30g flour, plus 3 tablespoons
3 tablespoons cocoa
½ teaspoon baking powder
½ teaspoon baking soda
¼ teaspoon salt
1 egg
2 tablespoons oil
120ml milk
½ teaspoon vanilla extract

Preparation:

1. Grease and flour a round baking pan. 2. In a medium bowl, stir together the sugar, flour, cocoa, baking powder, baking soda, and salt. 3. Add all other ingredients and beat with a wire whisk until smooth. 4. Pour batter into prepared pan. Place the pan in the basket, then insert the basket in Zone 1. The unit will default to Zone 1. Turn the dial to select BAKE, set the temperature to 165°C, and set the time to 20 minutes. 5. Bake until the toothpick inserted in the centre comes out clean or with crumbs clinging to it.

Homemade Custard

⏱ **Prep:** 10 minutes   🍲 **Cook:** 45 minutes   ❖ **Serves:** 6

Ingredients:

475ml whole milk
2 eggs
45g sugar
⅛ teaspoon salt
¼ teaspoon vanilla
Cooking spray
⅛ teaspoon nutmeg

Preparation:

1. In a blender, process milk, egg, sugar, salt, and vanilla until smooth. 2. Spray a round baking pan with nonstick spray and pour the custard into it. 3. Place the pan in the basket, then insert the basket in Zone 1. The unit will default to Zone 1. Turn the dial to select BAKE, set the temperature to 150°C, and set the time to 45 minutes. Custard is done when the centre sets. 4. Sprinkle top with the nutmeg. 5. Allow custard to cool slightly. 6. Serve it warm, at room temperature, or chilled.

Chocolate Chip Cookies

⏱ **Prep:** 5 minutes   🍲 **Cook:** 5 minutes   ❖ **Serves:** 8

Ingredients:

150g (2 sticks) unsalted butter, at room temperature
190g granulated sugar
190g brown sugar
2 large eggs
½ teaspoon vanilla extract
1 teaspoon baking soda
½ teaspoon salt
375g all-purpose flour
335g chocolate chips

Preparation:

1. Insert the crisper plates in the baskets and spray them with cooking spray. 2. In a large bowl, cream the butter and both sugars. 3. Mix in the eggs, vanilla, baking soda, salt, and flour until well combined. Fold in the chocolate chips. 4. Use your hands and knead the dough together, so everything is well mixed. 5. Using a cookie scoop or a tablespoon, drop heaping spoonfuls of dough onto each basket about 1 inch apart. 6. Then insert the baskets in the unit. The unit will default to Zone 1. Turn the dial to select BAKE. Set the temperature to 170°C and set the time to 5 minutes. Press the MATCH COOK button to copy Zone 1's settings to Zone 2. Press START/ PAUSE to begin cooking in both zones. 7. Let cool and serve.

Crunch S'mores

⏰ **Prep: 5 minutes**   🍲 **Cook: 3 minutes**   ≋ **Serves: 12**

Ingredients:

12 whole cinnamon graham crackers
2 (45g) chocolate bars, broken into 12 pieces
12 marshmallows

Preparation:

1. Halve each graham cracker into 2 squares. 2. Insert the crisper plates in the baskets. Arrange 6 graham cracker squares in each basket in one layer, place a piece of chocolate onto each. Then insert the baskets in the unit. The unit will default to Zone 1. Turn the dial to select BAKE. Set the temperature to 175°C and set the time to 2 minutes. Press the MATCH COOK button to copy Zone 1's settings to Zone 2. Press START/ PAUSE to begin cooking in both zones. 3. Open the air fryer and add a marshmallow onto each piece of melted chocolate. Cook for 1 additional minute. 4. Remove the cooked s'mores from the air fryer. Top with the remaining graham cracker squares and serve.

Chocolate-Frosted Doughnuts

⏰ **Prep: 5 minutes**   🍲 **Cook: 5 minutes**   ≋ **Serves: 8**

Ingredients:

1 (460g / 8-count) package refrigerated biscuit dough
90g powdered sugar
20g unsweetened cocoa powder
60ml milk

Preparation:

1. Unroll the biscuit dough onto a cutting board and separate the biscuits. 2. Using a 1-inch biscuit cutter or cookie cutter, cut out the centre of each biscuit. 3. Insert a crisper plate in the Zone 1 basket and spray with olive oil, arrange half of the doughnuts in a single layer in the basket. Then place one Stacked Meal Rack in the basket over the doughnuts. Place the remaining doughnuts on the rack, then insert the basket in the unit. 4. Select DOUBLE STACK PRO. Select Zone 1. Turn the dial to select BAKE, set the temperature to 165°C, and set the time to 5 minutes. Press START/PAUSE to begin cooking. 5. Using tongs, remove the doughnuts from the air fryer and let them cool slightly before glazing. 6. Meanwhile, in a small mixing bowl, combine the powdered sugar, unsweetened cocoa powder, and milk and mix until smooth. 7. Dip your doughnuts into the glaze and use a knife to smooth the frosting evenly over the doughnut. 8. Let the glaze set before serving.

Chapter 7 Desserts

Apple Hand Pies

⏲ **Prep: 15 minutes** 🍱 **Cook: 12 minutes** ◆ **Serves: 8**

Ingredients:

2 apples, cored and diced
85g honey
1 teaspoon cinnamon
1 teaspoon vanilla extract
⅛ teaspoon nutmeg
2 teaspoons cornstarch
1 teaspoon water
4 frozen piecrusts, thawed if frozen hard
Cooking oil

Preparation:

1. Place a saucepan over medium-high heat. Add the apples, honey, cinnamon, vanilla, and nutmeg. Stir and cook for 2 to 3 minutes, until the apples are soft. 2. In a small bowl, mix the cornstarch and water. Add to the pan and stir. Cook for 30 seconds. 3. Cut each piecrust into two 4-inch circles. You should have 8 circles of crust total. 4. Lay the piecrusts on a flat work surface. Mound ⅓ of the apple filling on the centre of each. 5. Fold each piecrust over so that the top layer of crust is about an inch short of the bottom layer. (The edges should not meet.)6. Using your fingers, tap along the edges of the top layer to seal. Use the back of a fork to press lines into the edges. 7. Insert a crisper plate in the Zone 1 basket, place 4 pies in a single layer in the basket, then place one Stacked Meal Rack in the basket over the pies. Place the remaining pies on the rack, then insert the basket in the unit. 8. Select DOUBLE STACK PRO. Select Zone 1. Turn the dial to select BAKE, set the temperature to 200°C, and set the time to 10 minutes. Press START/PAUSE to begin cooking. 9. Allow the hand pies to cool fully before removing from the air fryer.

Pumpkin Fritters

⏰ **Prep: 5 minutes**   🍲 **Cook: 8 minutes**   ❖ **Serves: 8**

Ingredients:

For the Fritters:
1 (460g, 8-count) package refrigerated biscuit dough
55g chopped pecans
60g pumpkin purée
45g sugar
1 teaspoon pumpkin pie spice
2 tablespoons unsalted butter, melted

For the Glaze:
235g powdered sugar
1 teaspoon pumpkin pie spice
1 tablespoon pumpkin purée
2 tablespoons milk (plus more to thin the glaze, if necessary)

Preparation:

To make the fritters: 1. Turn the biscuit dough out onto a cutting board. 2. Cut each biscuit into 8 pieces. 3. Once you cut all the pieces, place them in a medium mixing bowl. 4. Add the pecans, pumpkin, sugar, and pumpkin pie spice to the biscuit pieces and toss until well combined. 5. Shape the dough into 8 even mounds. 6. Drizzle butter over each of the fritters. (This will help them stay together as you air fry them.)7. Insert a crisper plate in the Zone 1 basket and spray with olive oil, place 4 fritters in a single layer in the basket, then place one Stacked Meal Rack in the basket over the fritters. Place the remaining fritters on the rack, then insert the basket in the unit. 8. Select DOUBLE STACK PRO. Select Zone 1. Turn the dial to select BAKE, set the temperature to 165°C, and set the time to 7 minutes. Press START/PAUSE to begin cooking. 9. Check to see if the fritters are done. The dough should be cooked through and solid to the touch. If not, cook for 1 to 2 minutes more. 10. Using tongs, gently remove the fritters from the air fryer. Let cool for about 10 minutes before you apply the glaze.

To make the glaze: 1. In a small mixing bowl, mix together the powdered sugar, pumpkin pie spice, pumpkin, and milk until smooth. If it seems more like icing, it is too thick. It should coat a spoon and be of a pourable consistency. 2. Drizzle the glaze over the fritters.

Conclusion

Thank you for exploring the Ninja DoubleStack XL 2-Basket Air Fryer Cookbook with us. We hope this culinary journey has equipped you with the knowledge and inspiration to make the most of your air fryer's capabilities. From crispy fries to succulent roasts and delightful desserts, this cookbook has offered a wide array of recipes to suit every palate and occasion.

As you continue to experiment with your Ninja DoubleStack XL, remember the convenience it brings to your kitchen with its dual-zone cooking, allowing you to prepare multiple dishes simultaneously without compromising on flavour or texture. Whether you're a seasoned chef or just starting out, the simplicity and efficiency of air frying can enhance your cooking experience.

Don't forget the importance of proper care and maintenance to ensure your air fryer remains in top condition for years to come. By following our cleaning tips and safety guidelines, you can enjoy delicious meals with peace of mind.

We hope this cookbook has sparked your creativity and encouraged you to explore new culinary horizons. Embrace the joy of healthier cooking and savour every moment with your Ninja DoubleStack XL 2-Basket Air Fryer. Happy cooking!

Appendix 1 Measurement Conversion Chart

VOLUME EQUIVALENTS (LIQUID)

US STANDARD	US STANDARD (OUNCES)	METRIC (APPROXIMATE)
2 tablespoons	1 fl.oz	30 mL
¼ cup	2 fl.oz	60 mL
½ cup	4 fl.oz	120 mL
1 cup	8 fl.oz	240 mL
1½ cup	12 fl.oz	355 mL
2 cups or 1 pint	16 fl.oz	475 mL
4 cups or 1 quart	32 fl.oz	1 L
1 gallon	128 fl.oz	4 L

TEMPERATURES EQUIVALENTS

FAHRENHEIT(F)	CELSIUS© (APPROXIMATE)
225 °F	107 °C
250 °F	120 °C
275 °F	135 °C
300 °F	150 °C
325 °F	160 °C
350 °F	180 °C
375 °F	190 °C
400 °F	205 °C
425 °F	220 °C
450 °F	235 °C
475 °F	245 °C
500 °F	260 °C

VOLUME EQUIVALENTS (DRY)

US STANDARD	METRIC (APPROXIMATE)
⅛ teaspoon	0.5 mL
¼ teaspoon	1 mL
½ teaspoon	2 mL
¾ teaspoon	4 mL
1 teaspoon	5 mL
1 tablespoon	15 mL
¼ cup	59 mL
½ cup	118 mL
¾ cup	177 mL
1 cup	235 mL
2 cups	475 mL
3 cups	700 mL
4 cups	1 L

WEIGHT EQUIVALENTS

US STANDARD	METRIC (APPROXINATE)
1 ounce	28 g
2 ounces	57 g
5 ounces	142 g
10 ounces	284 g
15 ounces	425 g
16 ounces (1 pound)	455 g
1.5 pounds	680 g
2 pounds	907 g

Appendix 2 Air Fryer Cooking Chart

Vegetables	Temp (°F)	Time (min)
Asparagus (1-inch slices)	400	5
Beets (sliced)	350	25
Beets (whole)	400	40
Bell Peppers (sliced)	350	13
Broccoli	400	6
Brussels Sprouts (halved)	380	15
Carrots (½-inch slices)	380	15
Cauliflower (florets)	400	12
Eggplant (1½-inch cubes)	400	15
Fennel (quartered)	370	15
Mushrooms (¼-inch slices)	400	5
Onion (pearl)	400	10
Parsnips (½-inch chunks)	380	5
Peppers (1-inch chunks)	400	15
Potatoes (baked, whole)	400	40
Squash (½-inch chunks)	400	12
Tomatoes (cherry)	400	4
Zucchni (½-inch sticks)	400	12

Meat	Temp (°F)	Time (min)
Bacon	400	5 to 7
Beef Eye Round Roast (4 lbs.)	390	50 to 60
Burger (4 oz.)	370	16 to 20
Chicken Breasts, bone-in (1.25 lbs.)	370	25
Chicken Breasts, boneless (4 oz.)	380	12
Chicken Drumsticks (2.5 lbs.)	370	20
Chicken Thighs, bone-in (2 lbs.)	380	22
Chicken Thighs, boneless (1.5 lbs.)	380	18 to 20
Chicken Legs, bone-in (1.75 lbs.)	380	30
Chicken Wings (2 lbs.)	400	12
Flank Steak (1.5 lbs.)	400	12
Game Hen (halved, 2 lbs.)	390	20
Loin (2 lbs.)	360	55
London Broil (2 lbs.)	400	20 to 28
Meatballs (3-inch)	380	10
Rack of Lamb (1.5-2 lbs.)	380	22
Sausages	380	15
Whole Chicken (6.5 lbs.)	360	75

Fish and Seafood	Temp (°F)	Time (min)
Calamari (8 oz.)	400	4
Fish Fillet (1-inch, 8 oz.)	400	10
Salmon Fillet (6 oz.)	380	12
Tuna Steak	400	7 to 10
Scallops	400	5 to 7
Shrimp	400	5

Frozen Foods	Temp (°F)	Time (min)
Onion Rings (12 oz.)	400	8
Thin French Fries (20 oz.)	400	14
Thick French Fries (17 oz.)	400	18
Pot Sticks (10 oz.)	400	8
Fish Sticks (10 oz.)	400	10
Fish Fillets (½-inch, 10 oz.)	400	14

Appendix 3 Recipes Index

A

Air Fryer Chicken Drumsticks with Honey BBQ Sauce 37

Air Fryer Mexican Street Corn 19

Air-Fried Chicken Wings 28

Air-Fried Eggs 12

Almond-Baked Pears 58

Apple Hand Pies 62

Apple-Walnut Muffins 14

Authentic Carne Asada 47

B

BBQ Chicken Wings 32

Beef Sliders 48

Beef-Rice Stuffed Peppers 53

Beer-Battered Cod and Chips 42

Blueberry Pancake Poppers 16

Buffalo Chicken Bites 31

Buffalo Chicken Egg Rolls 34

Bulgogi Burgers with Gochujang Mayonnaise 52

Buttermilk-Fried Chicken Drumsticks 35

C

Cheese Corn Dip 30

Cheese Meatballs and Potatoes 51

Cheese Sausage Pizzas 30

Cheese-Bacon Stuffed Potatoes 24

Chinese-Style Baby Back Ribs 46

Chocolate Chip Cookies 60

Chocolate-Frosted Doughnuts 61

Classic Natchitoches Meat Pie 56

Classic Scotch Eggs 15

Coriander-Lime Shrimp 41

Corn on the Cob 23

Crisp Apple Chips 29

Crisp Bacon 14

Crisp Yuca Fries 20

Crispy Brussels Sprouts with Mustard Aioli 23

Crispy Chicken Cutlets with Spaghetti 36

Crispy Corn Tortilla Chips 31

Crispy Fish Sticks 40

Crunch S'mores 61

Crunchy Chicken and Ranch Tortillas 37

Crunchy Chicken Chunks 35

Crunchy French Fries with Toum 26

Crunchy Kale Chips 29

Crunchy Potato Fries 21

Cumin Pork Tenderloin and Potatoes 45

D

Dark Brownies 59

Delicious Firecracker Shrimp 43

F

Falafel with Cucumber-Tomato Salad 25

Flavourful Kofta Kebabs 46

Fluffy Chocolate Cake 59

G

Garlic Butter Toast 13

Garlic Green Beans 19

Garlicky Chicken Wings 38

H

Herbed Polenta Fries 18

Herb-Stuffed Potatoes 22

Hoisin Barbecue Country-Style Pork Ribs 50

Home-Fried Potatoes and Peppers 16

Homemade Buttermilk Biscuits 13

Homemade Custard 60

Homemade Hush Puppies 18

I

Italian Cheese Sausage Meatballs 47

J

Juicy Teriyaki Chicken Legs 34

L

Lamb Kofta with Tzatziki 45

M

Mint Lamb Kebabs 49

N

Nutty Whole Wheat Muffins 15

P

Pecan-Stuffed Apple 58

Pumpkin Fritters 63

R

Roasted Cherry Tomatoes with Basil 20

S

Salty and Sweet Salmon 41

Savoury Meatballs with Marinara 50

Savoury Salmon Croquettes 42

Soft Banana Bread 12

Sonoran Style Hot Dogs 55

Spiced Carrots 21

Spicy Cajun Shrimp 43

Spicy Pork Bulgogi 49

Spinach and Cream Cheese Stuffed Chicken 38

Steamboat Shrimp and Tomato Salad 40

Sweet & Spicy Chicken Wings 32

Sweet & Spicy Walnuts 28

T

Teriyaki Baby Back Ribs 54

The Best Steak Frites 48

Turkey-Hummus Cheese Wraps 36

Y

Yummy Sweet Potato Fries 22

Printed in Great Britain
by Amazon